PAM GEMS

Plays Five

PAM GEMS

Plays Five

THE BLUE ANGEL

LOVING WOMEN

NATALYA

LADYBIRD, LADYBIRD

Q
QUOTA BOOKS LTD
LONDON

Published in 2022 by Quota Books Ltd.
197 Hammersmith Grove, London W6 0NP
website: www.quotabooks.com – email: info@quotabooks.com
Twitter: @Quotabooks

Copyright © Pam Gems

Pam Gems is identified as the Author of the Work in accordance with Section 7 of the Copyright, Designs and Patents Act 1988. The author has asserted her moral rights.

All rights whatsoever in these plays are strictly reserved and application for performance etc. should be made before commencement of rehearsals to Rose Cobbe, United Agents, 12–26 Lexington Street, London W1F 0LE, UK. info@unitedagents.co.uk Tel: +44 (0) 20 3214 0800.

No performance may be given unless a licence has been obtained.

This book is sold subject to the condition that it shall not, by way of trade or otherwise, be lent, resold, hired out or otherwise circulated without the publisher's prior consent in any form of binding or cover other than that in which it is published and without a similar condition, including this condition, being imposed on the subsequent publisher.

A CIP record for this book is available from the British Library.

ISBN 978-1-7398894-0-1

Typeset in the UK by M Rules
Printed and bound by Biddles
Picture of Pam Gems courtesy of Jonathan Gems
Cover design: TRISTAN

Available from Amazon, Ingram Spark, Quota Books
and all politically correct bookstores.

Pam Gems was born in 1925 in Mudeford, near Christchurch, in what was then Dorset, on the south coast of England. Her father, a Welsh ex-coalminer, died when she was six years old, leaving her mother to bring up Pam and her two brothers on her own.

For most of her childhood, Pam's family lived in poverty, reliant on charity from the parish church and the Salvation Army. At eleven, she won a scholarship to grammar school, where she flourished, but left at fifteen to go to work.

World War Two broke out and, in 1943 (when she turned eighteen), she joined the Women's Royal Naval Service, and worked with British and Canadian bomber squadrons. She writes about this in FINCHIE's WAR. After the war, she went to Manchester University, where she studied psychology and met her future husband, Keith.

Always stage-struck, Gems wrote her first play when she was eight, and was an enthusiastic participant in school plays. At university, she joined the dramatic society, wrote skits, produced and directed. After university, she worked in audience research at the BBC – which she loathed – and became part of the 'Ban the Bomb' London beatnik scene, which included Ted Hughes, the poet, Sean Kenny, the designer, and Robert Bolt, the playwright.

After marrying and having her first two children, she and her husband moved to Wandsworth in South London, where she wrote radio plays, beginning a prolific writing career that produced over seventy plays and adaptations. Pam Gems is, without doubt, Britain's greatest woman dramatist, with only Agatha Christie having had more West End productions.

Agatha Christie had ten plays presented in the West End, at a time when the economics of West End plays weren't as prohibitive as they later became. Pam Gems had six, arguably seven, West End plays. The first was DUSA FISH STAS and VI, at the Mayfair, presented by Michael Codron, followed by PIAF, at the Piccadilly, presented by the RSC, which also produced CAMILLE at the Comedy, and THE BLUE ANGEL at the Globe. LOVING WOMEN was presented at the Arts Theatre, and MARLENE had a successful run at the Lyric. STANLEY, which played to full houses at the National Theatre, was offered a West-End transfer by three managements, but the company preferred to transfer to the Circle in the Square, off-Broadway, in New York, where the play ran for six months.

One thing that especially fascinates in Pam Gems' writing is the prophetic element. She perceived, well in advance, the dangers facing the pampered and decadent West, which we now see unfolding. As Victor Hugo said: 'Adversity makes men and prosperity makes monsters.' Her approach is always positive, however. Like the Beatles' song, all you need is love.

Jonathan Gems

ALSO BY THE SAME AUTHOR

Betty's Wonderful Christmas
Go West Young Woman
Queen Christina
Piaf
Camille
Pasionaria
Deborah's Daughter
Marlene
Stanley
The Snow Palace
King Ludwig of Bavaria
Mrs. Pat
Ethel
Not Joan the Musical
The Socialists
Dusa, Fish, Stas, and Vi
At the Window
Aunt Mary

Garibaldi, Si!
The Incorruptible
The Treat
Franz Into April
Up in Sweden
Next Please
My Warren
The Amiable Courtship of Miz Venus and Wild Bill
The Synonym
The Whippet
The Russian Princess
The Burning Man
A Builder by Trade
The Nourishing Lie
Mr Watts
In Donegal
Cluster
Down West

The Country House Sale
In The Hothouse
Guin for Guinevere
Marine
Who Is Sylvia?
The Project
You Should Be Pleased He Likes Me
What Luck
An Ordinary Woman
We Never Do What They Want
Stella Campbell
Finchie's War
The Leg-Up
Maytime
Mabel's Bistro
A Kind of Ecstasy

ADAPTATIONS

Sarah B Divine!
My Name is Rosa Luxemburg
Rivers and Forests
Darling Boy
Uncle Vanya
A Doll's House

Stanley's Women
The Seagull
Ghosts
Yerma
The Lady from the Sea
The Cherry Orchard
The Dance of Death

The Father
Hedda Gabbler
Three Sisters
The Odd Women
The Little Mermaid
Behaving Badly

NOVELS

Mrs Frampton
Bon Voyage, Mrs Frampton

CONTENTS

THE BLUE ANGEL	1
LOVING WOMEN	135
NATALYA	263
LADYBIRD, LADYBIRD	363

THE BLUE ANGEL

By Pam Gems
from the novel 'Professor Unraat'
by Heinrich Mann

For Trevor Nunn

THE BLUE ANGEL was first performed on the 7th of September, 1991 at The Other Place, Stratford-Upon-Avon, Warwickshire. The production transferred to the Globe Theatre, London, on the 20th of May, 1992. Produced by MARK FURNESS, JOHN NEWMAN and the Royal Shakespeare Company, directed by TREVOR NUNN, designed by MARIA BJORNSON.

CAST

Lola	KELLY HUNTER
Professor Raat	PHILIP MADOC
Mai Bombler	JUDITH BRUCE
Friedrich Bombler	SIDNEY LIVINGSTONE
Dieter	PETER HUGO DALY
TumTum	CHERYL FERGISON
Berthe	SARAH FLIND
Klaus	JULIAN FORSYTH
Paul	PATRICK TOOMEY
Hermine	JACKIE EKERS
Cobbler/Dutch Captain/ Janitor/Dr Lippmann/Judge	DESMOND McNAMARA
Hans/Herr Pressman	CHARLES SIMPSON
Lutz/Policeman	JONATHAN WEIR
Frau Pflug/Hat-Check Girl/ Cobbler's Wife Hannaliese	ARHLENE ALLAN
Headmaster/Mayor	ALLAN MITCHELL
Policeman	MICHAEL SANDERSON
Understudies	KIM BARRY
	GERALD HOME
	PETER WHITFIELD

Choreographer	DAVID TOGURI
Musical Director, Musical Arrangements and Additional Music by	STEVEN EDIS
Lighting by	CHRIS PARRY
Sound by	STEVEN BROWN
Assistant Director	WILLIAM JAMES
Production Manager	CARO MACKAY
Wardrobe Supervisor	ALLAN WATKINS
Production Electrician	ALISTER GRANT
Stage Manager	DONNA WIFFEN
Deputy Stage Manager	EMMA TURNER
Assistant Stage Manager	DANNY BURROUGH
Sound Operators	FERGUS O'HARE
	ADELE FURNESS
Wardrobe Mistress	ANNETTE HERON
Deputy Wardrobe Mistress	ANJA GAHMANN
Wig Mistress	SARA TAYLOR
Assistant Lighting Designer	CHARLOTTE McCLELLAND
Dressers	MARIA KIRBY
	YVETTE GLOVER
Photographer	CLIVE BARDA

REVIEWS

Pam Gems has based this musical play on Heinrich Mann's 1905 novel, *Professor Unraat*. But she has updated the action to Hamburg in the late 1920s and incorporated Friedrich Hollander's songs from Sternberg's legendary 1930s film. The result, however, is much more savage than the movie.

It is still the story of a middle-aged schoolteacher hopelessly enthralled by a chanteuse. But Lola, here, is clearly a working whore. Rejected by the Hamburg bourgeoisie for marrying her, Professor Raat turns into a thriving blackmailer and, where the film's final image of him in clown make-up crowing like a cock is equivocal in that it acknowledges his animality, here there is no doubt as to his total moral degradation in pursuit of a phantom love.

As a study in erotic obsession, the play packs a considerable punch. It also gives the story a political dimension I don't remember from the film.

Indeed, it becomes an almost Brechtian fable, echoing The Threepenny Opera, in which the rapacity and corruption of the Weimar bourgeoisie is precisely mirrored by the lewd chicanery of the show-folk. The two worlds even merge in a series of wittily-staged scenes, where the disgraced Professor uses Lola as bait to blackmail her lovers, which are presented as if they were episodic vignettes from the Blue Angel cabaret.

Where it succeeds as a piece of theatre, however, is in rubbing our noses in the tacky vulgarity of the cabaret while also allowing us guiltily to enjoy it ...

Trevor Nunn's superb production works because it never lets us forget that the Blue Angel is a distorted mirror-image of the Weimar Republic. And Maria Bjornson's marvellous composite set makes the point visually by allowing the cabaret to erupt on the twisty, tram-lined, cobbled streets of a miniaturized Hamburg.

MICHAEL BILLINGTON. *The Guardian*. 28/08/1991

The new Other Place opened in Stratford-upon-Avon on Thursday night with Trevor Nunn's production for the Royal Shakespeare Company of THE BLUE ANGEL by Pam Gems ...

It is fitting that the RSC's wunderkind, turned eminence grise, should return to launch it with a hypnotically double-edged fable on the pleasure principle ...

But, in returning to Heinrich Mann's 1905 novel, Professor Unraat, Nunn and Gems reveal a much harsher story and extend the Expressionist references right back to Wedekind. Lola is a focus for adolescent fixation, and it is the determination of the schoolmaster to expunge Lola's evil influence that leads to his own sexual enslavement and downfall ...

Kelly Hunter, in a fabulous wardrobe of skimpy underwear, creates an intriguing mixture of siren and victim, of ruthlessness and generosity, that is a complex and estimable addition to the Pam Gems roster of legendary pin-ups: Piaf, Camille and Queen Christina ...

MICHAEL COVENEY. *Financial Times*. 01/09/1991

The curtain rises on Stratford's revamped third theatre ... The first production is in the hands of Trevor Nunn, who presided over the opening of the original Other Place, and the play is Pam Gems's THE BLUE ANGEL, adapted from Heinrich Mann's famous novel of 1905, *Professor Unraat*.

Actually, 'adapted' is not quite the right word. Gems has relocated the story to 1920s Hamburg and Maria Bjornson's set, with its precipitous angles and lurid doorways, recalls the films of Murnau. The atmosphere is cool but febrile. The characters might have stepped out of the canvases of Beckmann or Dix.

Mann's tale of an elderly schoolmaster's infatuation with a cabaret singer is a study in the pathology of repression. Herr Raat (Philip Madoc, fierce, dignified, vulnerable) is a savage disciplinarian ... Lola is destructive because she knows no law except survival. Raat is doomed because he knows nothing but law and order.

Gems has seized on the prophetic aspect of Mann's story for, already in 1905, Mann could sense that unthinking discipline would, in the long run, undermine and corrupt the moral fibre of disciplinarians. And so, where Mann led Raat into the degradation of squalor, Gems leads him into the more profound degradation of corruption ...

Kelly Hunter's Lola is both victim and predator, athletic and defenceless. This is a star performance, full of pain, pride and poise. The eyes are vacuous but intense, alive to every noise and movement in the jungle. On stage, she is lean, coltish, a remote but provocative thoroughbred. You can see that, to Raat, she holds the possibility of thrilling mutual submission. In her tatty dressing-gown she relaxes, almost shrinks, into vulnerability and the wariness of a child who has never been loved. She is not Mann's almost passive figure of temptation, but a successor to Gems's Piaf and Camille: a bruised but proud victim of a predatory society.

JOHN PETERS. *The Sunday Times.* 01/09/1991

THE BLUE ANGEL

CAST

LOLA
PROFESSOR IMMANUEL RAAT
FRIEDRICH BOMBLER
MAI, his wife
HERMINE, their daughter
BERTHA
TUMTUM
KLAUS, strong man
DIETER, clown
DUTCH CAPTAIN
HANS
PAUL, Baron von Eberhardt
LUTZ
HEADMASTER
JANITOR
FRAU PFLUG
JUDGE
MAYOR
HERR PRESSMAN
POLICEMAN
WAITER
DOKTOR LIPPMANN
HANNALIESE (LIESEL)
COBBLER
COBBLER'S WIFE
WOMAN OF THE STREETS
WAITRESS

THE BLUE ANGEL

ACT ONE

ACT ONE. SCENE ONE.

The Blue Angel nightclub.

The sounds of a BAND tuning up, with loud brass sounds dominant.

Suddenly the TROUPE erupts onstage.

DIETER carries a small violin and mimes in ecstasy.

KLAUS, the strong man, bends bars.

HERR BOMBLER, the manager, does conjuring tricks, assisted by MAI, his wife, and HERMINE, his adolescent daughter.

BERTHA and TUMTUM (two fat girls), do a tap dance, getting in everyone's way, and stopping unselfconsciously to get their breath.

HERMINE drops something.

BERTHA holds her side as she gets a stitch.

BOMBLER, finishing despite HERMINE, signs for DIETER to wrap KLAUS in chains.

> BOMBLER
> Hoop-la! ... and Hoop-La! *(He crosses, and mutters to MAI)* Where's Lola?
>
> MAI
> *(Grabbing a quick gin.)* How the devil should I know?

MAI hurtles back onstage.

BOMBLER crosses to the dressing area. He grabs a bag of large buns from the table, and thrusts the bag at BERTHA.

BOMBLER

Come on, you two. Eat up!

BERTHA

(*Hoarse*) Oh, not again, Guv!

TUMTUM

(*Takes a bun obediently*) We'll get fat, Uncle.

BOMBLER lifts his eyes heavenwards, and snatches the bag away from HERMINE.

BOMBLER

(*To TUMTUM*) You lose weight, you lose your job.
Where's Lola?

DIETER, as the routine ends, crosses to the dressing area as the BAND plays loudly and KLAUS breaks his chains.

DIETER looks offstage at BOMBLER's request.

BOMBLER

Give her a shout.

DIETER looks at him blankly.

BOMBLER

What are you waiting for?

DIETER goes.

BOMBLER

Is he deaf as well as dumb?

TUMTUM

Uncle Fred, don't ...

ACT ONE

HERMINE

Daddy!

BERTHA

Come on, guv, you know how Dieter feels about Lola.

BOMBLER

More fool him ... Oh, no ...

Three students, PAUL, HANS and LUTZ wander in.

TUMTUM and HERMINE squeal. BERTHA tries to shove the boys out genially.

PAUL smiles as HANS evades the girls. He flops onto a basket and ostentatiously lights a cigarette.

HANS

Miss Lola in yet?

BOMBLER

She's just about to sing, sir. Now you won't want to miss her.

The STUDENTS go.

BOMBLER bows to PAUL who leaves, followed by BERTHA and TUMTUM, who clearly find Paul attractive.

They collide with MAI.

MAI

Where the hell is Lola? They're starting to leave already!

BOMBLER

Put the elephants on. *(To HERMINE)* Not you.

He regards HERMINE, who has two pigtails and glasses, and lifts his head skywards in disgust.

BOMBLER

Look, do something! Pull your hair over your face.

HERMINE

(As he tries to pull at her hair) Daddy!

BOMBLER

I'm doing your mother a favour. You're not a good-looking girl.

BERTHA and TUMTUM sing 'Morgens Einen, Mittags Einen, Abends Einen Kuss,' and dance with beach balls, calling to the audience. Shouts for them to get off.

Prolonged shouts for Lola.

Light change.

ACT ONE – SCENE TWO.

A Schoolroom.

Present are HANS, LUTZ and PAUL.

The noise in the classroom stops as PROFESSOR RAAT appears, papers under his arm. He glares round at the class, takes out his handkerchief without haste, and blows his nose, sniffing heavily.

HANS
(Sotto voce) Funny smell in here.

LUTZ
(Sotto voce) Must be the drains.

HANS
(Sotto voce) Perhaps there's a sewer rat somewhere.

The PROFESSOR glowers suspiciously. He gives out the essays.

ACT ONE

PROFESSOR

Schelling. *(He throws HANS' essay onto his desk.)*
Rubbish. Eisendorf. *(He hits LUTZ over the head
with his essay, then throws it down.)* Illiterate and
incompetent rubbish! Von Eberhardt.

PAUL looks up hopefully to receive his essay but the PROFESSOR retains it. Silence. He addresses the class.

PROFESSOR

It is my considered belief that none of you ... not one
of you ... has reached the standard which would
secure, beyond doubt, a university entrance.

He throws PAUL's essay at him violently, making him duck.

PROFESSOR

Eberhardt. Scurrilous, inflammatory and
impertinent rubbish.

PAUL masks his disappointment.

PAUL

(Politely) I'm sorry you found it so, sir.

PROFESSOR

Was that not your intention?

Silence.

PAUL picks up his essay. A paper falls from his desk.

The PROFESSOR picks it up. He makes to hand it back, then, as an afterthought, turns it over, and reads it.

PROFESSOR

What is this?

PAUL

A verse, sir.

PROFESSOR

(Raps) Subject?

PAUL

(Pause) It's personal, sir.

Then the PROFESSOR reads aloud.

PROFESSOR

Lithe, not lean is her L.
O connotes ordinary,
No, never ... Overwhelming!
L once more, Level-eyed,
Laughing ...
And A?
A is for adoration.
Mmm. Personal. 'Lithe, not lean is her L' ... L ... L ...
O ... *(He mutters)* ... L – O – L – A?

PAUL

It spells Lola.

PROFESSOR

And who is this ... Lola?

Silence.

PROFESSOR

Schelling!

HANS

An actress, sir.

PROFESSOR

(Turning on PAUL, gleaming.) An actress!

HANS

(Quickly) At the Classical Theatre, sir. Playing Racine. Or it might be Corneille.

ACT ONE

LUTZ

Or Moliere.

HANS

Or the Greeks.

The PROFESSOR, baulked, turns to PAUL, sourly.

But PAUL has gone to open the door.

Enter the HEADMASTER.

There is instant silence.

HEADMASTER

Thank you, boy.

The HEADMASTER draws the PROFESSOR apart.

HEADMASTER

Forgive the interruption. I simply wanted to say, Raat, your new syllabus is a triumph. Sound work!

PROFESSOR

Thank you, headmaster.

HEADMASTER

(His eye falls on PAUL, standing politely by the door.)
Ah, young von Eberhardt. Another credit to you.
Exemplary behaviour. It's in the family, of course.

PROFESSOR

(Through his teeth) He is always most polite.

The HEADMASTER gives a friendly nod and exits.

Silence.

A HAND BELL RINGS, offstage. The BOYS stand to attention.

PROFESSOR

Move to assembly, in alphabetical order. Eberhardt.

PAUL remains, standing to attention.

> PROFESSOR
>
> There was no need, Baron von Eberhardt (*He stresses PAUL's name sarcastically*) for you to take the blame for Eisendorf's foolishness in the corridor. Remember, if you will, that here you are no more than any other boy.

PAUL makes to answer

> PROFESSOR
>
> Dismissed.

PAUL turns to go.

> PROFESSOR
>
> And who is this actress, that you write verses for her?

PAUL remains silent.

> PROFESSOR
>
> You may, Eberhardt, blind our good headmaster with fine behaviour and a superior manner. You may also care to remember that I, your Professor, see through you.

PAUL exits.

> PROFESSOR
>
> The Classical Theatre plays only in summer. We are in winter now! (*He crushes the paper with the poem triumphantly. Then he flattens it out.*) Lola ... Lola ... (*He chuckles triumphantly.*) At last, Eberhardt, I think we may have you!

He exits.

ACT ONE

The BOYS erupt across the stage, taking their chairs with them, laughing and yelling.

HANS

Corneille ... Racine!

LUTZ

She's playing Helen of Troy!

HANS

In a shimmy, sir!

Light change.

ACT ONE - SCENE THREE.

A Dark Street and an open Cobbler's Shop.

In the back, the COBBLER'S WIFE brings on the evening meal. TWO CHILDREN are seated expectantly at the table.

The COBBLER steps forward.

COBBLER

I had always made the Professor's boots, although I hadn't seen him – thanks to my own good work – for some time. Not until this evening ...

He retreats, for his meal.

WIFE

Potatoes, Fritz?

COBBLER

Thank you, Hedwig.

WIFE

They're very good tonight.

COBBLER

They're very good every night.

The PROFESSOR enters, looking about him for street signs.

He crosses the stage and the COBBLER, seeing him, wipes his mouth and rises, wiping his hands on his apron.

He holds up the candle.

COBBLER

Herr Professor! How may I help you?

PROFESSOR

Good evening, Stein. Ah ... be so good as to measure me for a new pair of boots.

COBBLER

Certainly, sir.

WIFE

You take the light, Professor. The children can eat in the dark.

The PROFESSOR sits.

The COBBLER kneels before him with his measure.

PROFESSOR

Stein ... I am looking for ... for ... Are there theatres in this quarter?

COBBLER

(*Amazed*) Theatres, Herr Professor?

PROFESSOR

I thought not. I am in search of an errant student and I have reason to believe that he is frequenting ... (*He looks about, as if seeking PAUL in the shadows.*)

ACT ONE

COBBLER

No, sir ... nothing like that. Not your sort of ... There *is* entertainment ...

PROFESSOR

Where?

COBBLER

Which our church has frequently tried to close down.

PROFESSOR

Where?

COBBLER

Beer cellars, sir. That way, sir. Down by the docks.

WIFE

Would the Professor honour us? We've plenty to spare.

She snatches the plates back from the CHILDREN.

COBBLER

But you couldn't be seen there, Herr Professor.

PROFESSOR

I beg your pardon? Be good enough not to offer me irrelevant observations.

He strides off.

The COBBLER makes after him, pointing directions, and stops.

Behind him, his WIFE blunders about in the dark.

The PROFESSOR crosses the stage, finding his way.

A WOMAN calls seductively from a doorway.

WOMAN

You're a fine-looking man. Upstanding you look.

The PROFESSOR jumps, and hurries on.

> WOMAN
> No need to hurry away. (*Slight pause*) Go on, piss off, you mouldering old shit.

The sound of VOICES calling for Lola.

The PROFESSOR hesitates, veers.

The sounds become louder. The PROFESSOR makes towards them.

He reaches an entrance. Over the door is the sign 'The Blue Angel.'

From inside the calls for Lola get louder.

The PROFESSOR pauses. He is drawn to a large poster in a self-standing frame by the entrance. It is a large picture of Lola.

He bends and peers at it. Then he straightens up ... and marches into the club.

ACT ONE – SCENE FOUR.

The Blue Angel.

Blue smoke and LOUD CALLS for Lola.

She appears with her back to us. She turns and breaks into '*My Name is Naughty Lola.*'

During the orchestra break, she saunters back and forth, inspecting her audience.

> LOLA
> What's the matter, boys? Feeling lonely? What do you want?

Shouts of: "You!" "What do you think?" "A good time!"

ACT ONE

LOLA

No – really? *(She laughs, a low, infectious laugh.)*
Why can't you learn to wait? I'm not interested in
fast workers. Where does that leave Lola? Let's have
a look. *(She peruses her audience, wetting her lower
lip.)* One or two ... promising situations. Hang on,
boys. Don't chew the upholstery! Lola's here.

Cheers and whistles. She finishes the song, then walks off and flops in the Dressing Room.

MAI, HERMINE, BERTHA and TUMTUM take over onstage.

BOMBLER brings LOLA a stein of beer. She drinks it straight down.

BOMBLER

That's my girl! *(He closes on her amorously.)* My God,
Lola, I'd do anything for you.

LOLA

Good. How about a raise?

BOMBLER

Anything! *(He drops on his knees, clutching and
kissing her.)* You're driving me out of my mind!

LOLA

Come in, boys.

BOMBLER scrambles to his feet, as HANS, LUTZ and PAUL enter.

For a brief moment, PAUL and LOLA grin across BOMBLER'S head, finding the moment hilarious. Then PAUL turns away.

BOMBLER

Not now, sir. The artistes are busy.

LOLA

Oh, go on. Their money's good. Makes a change, see someone young.

BOMBLER scowls and goes.

HANS and LUTZ descend on LOLA. PAUL stands further off, watching.

She lifts her legs lazily.

LUTZ takes them in his lap and reverently takes off her shoes. She lifts a stockinged foot in the silence.

LUTZ bends and reverently kisses the top of her instep.

PAUL

(Murmurs) Fabulous.

She looks across at PAUL and he turns away. He turns back sharply as HANS leans forward and makes to touch her breasts.

She waves PAUL away, and hits HANS, elegantly but hard, with her hairbrush.

HANS

Ow!

LOLA laughs.

LOLA

Are you all in tonight?

PAUL

Half the class.

LOLA

Good. Tell them to drink up. It keeps the guvnor sweet. *(She leans forward to LUTZ, murmurs)* What's the matter?

ACT ONE

He closes his eyes in ecstasy as she shakes his hand to and fro gently. She kisses his palm and folds it over, looking at PAUL all the time.

LOLA

(To LUTZ) Don't wash that for a week. *(She locks glances with PAUL, who turns away.)* And don't worry about it. About anything. I don't.

LUTZ

(Doleful) I'll never make Heidelberg.

PAUL

You will.

LUTZ

He'll fail me.

HANS

The Sewer Rat? Not in his interest.

LOLA

Sewer Rat? Why'd you call him that?

The BOYS look at one another, laughing.

PAUL

Because he's mad.

HANS

A sadist, you mean.

DIETER comes in. He jerks his head for the BOYS to go, and stands, glowering.

HANS

Paul, you coming?

HANS and LUTZ leave the Dressing Room to watch KLAUS lift enormous weights.

PAUL returns DIETER'S cold stare.

DIETER backs down, and exits.

> PAUL
> I've written something for you.

> LOLA
> Oh?

> PAUL
> Shall I read it?

> LOLA
> *(Indifferently)* What's it about? *(She turns away, occupied with her stockings.)*

> PAUL
> *(Rebuffed, he puts the paper in his pocket.)* It doesn't matter. Sorry to have bothered you.

> LOLA
> You don't bother me.

> PAUL
> No?

> LOLA
> Not in the least.

They are close. He looks down at her, and is satisfied. He puts the verse down gently on her table.

The SOUND OF SHOUTING. LUTZ and HANS run in quickly.

> PROFESSOR
> *(Offstage)* Come back here, you boys! Come back, I say! I see you! I see you! You will not escape!

> HANS
> It's the Sewer Rat! ... Professor Raat!

ACT ONE

PROFESSOR

(Offstage) Please allow me to pass! There is no mistake. I saw them! Be good enough to allow me through if you please! Out of my way!

LOLA waves the students upstairs. They hop up and out of sight.

PROFESSOR RAAT enters at a rush, pushing past DIETER, who tries to stop him.

He is followed by BOMBLER.

BOMBLER

Not in there, sir ...

PROFESSOR

I must insist! I saw them come in here. Oh!

He is exposed to LOLA, who is not fully clothed.

PROFESSOR

I beg your pardon!

But he cannot take his eyes off her.

BOMBLER

With the greatest respect, sir. If you wouldn't mind leaving for the moment ...

LOLA

Not at all. Come in.

PROFESSOR

(Gapes, attempts to recover.) I am looking for three of my students. I have reason to believe they came ...

LOLA

Here? *(Looks round, hand to breast in pretty alarm.)* In here? Why, are they playing truant? Surely these are not school hours?

PROFESSOR

It is my duty to supervise the moral welfare of my pupils at all times. They have important examinations ahead of them.

BOMBLER shoves DIETER on to perform.

MAI and the GIRLS enter.

BOMBLER

Right, straight into 'Blondes' with the new intro. *(To HERMINE)* Not you.

HERMINE

Daddy!

MAI

Yes, she does.

BOMBLER

(To MAI) No!

LOLA

(Calls across the melée) We're very honoured.

HERMINE

Can I wear the wings?

BOMBLER

I've told you, stay off!

HERMINE

Mutti!

MAI

Never mind, darling. He's horrible.

LOLA

(Sweetly, ignoring the fracas) It's not often we get a visit from a personage of such status.

ACT ONE

The GIRLS hurtle 'onstage' followed by BOMBLER, MAI and HERMINE. Peace reigns.

LOLA

Can we offer you something? A drop of S-h-a-m?

PROFESSOR

(Puzzled) Sham?

LOLA

Champagne?

PROFESSOR

Oh, you mean *C*-h-a-m ...

He makes to correct her spelling, but her hand touches his as she hands him a glass. She lifts her own glass charmingly and drinks to him.

He puts down his glass without drinking.

PROFESSOR

I must ask for your cooperation, please.

LOLA

(Murmurs) Boys will be boys, Professor. For you it's different. You're a mature man, experienced. I can see that. They are so lucky to have you to guide them. Would you be so kind? *(She indicates a garment hanging on a screen. He reacts, but takes it down and hands it to her.)* Thank you so much.

She goes behind the screen. The STUDENTS, getting a marvellous view of her, are excited, watching her change.

LOLA

(Calls) What a nice town you have. So charming. The river, very nice ... er, nice trees ...

PROFESSOR

We have here the finest biological specimens in Germany.

LOLA leans out, mouths an 'Ooh!'

PROFESSOR

And a very extensive library.

LOLA

(Calls) Never! Could you hold these a minute?

She hands him a pair of pink frilly knickers.

Enter KLAUS, out of temper, followed by BOMBLER.

BOMBLER

Klaus, what are we going to do about that bloody python?

KLAUS

Look, just don't talk to me like that!

BOMBLER

Oh God. I'm sorry, but...

KLAUS

He's a bit off colour, that's all. Just don't upset me.

Enter BERTHA, TUMTUM, MAI and HERMINE.

BOMBLER

Come on, skirts up! *(He gropes TUMTUM who squeals.)*

TUMTUM

Uncle!

The GIRLS grab new props, and change hats.

ACT ONE

BOMBLER

Come on, come on ... (*He hustles them out.*)

They all go.

LOLA emerges, transformed.

LOLA

There! Do you prefer me like this?

PROFESSOR

Really, my dear lady, I could not say. I am here on a serious errand. I saw them. I know he's here. I recognised the school uniform. To wear it in such a place! Vileness.

LOLA puts on a decorous but fetching dressing gown.

LOLA

Mein liebe Herr. Try not to think too harshly of us. This is a seagoing town! The men who come here for a few hours of ... ah ... respite. They're far from home. They are lonely.

He flicks a glance at her. She has caught his raw spot.

PROFESSOR

There is always the YMCA.

LOLA

Of course. But a beer or two, a song ... The way of the people, Herr Professor. Simple repose for honest young men who, alas, have not the good fortune to be counted among your students.

PROFESSOR

They will certainly not have been guided by a code of proper conduct.

LOLA

Seafaring men. Rough and ready, true. But good Germans.

PROFESSOR

I agree. I accept that.

LOLA

The sea is a cruel mistress. Would you?

She hands him her make-up to hold while she dips in, making up her face. This makes him flustered, but he obeys from politeness.

PROFESSOR

I am myself devoted to the works of Josef Conrad.

LOLA

Absolutely.

PROFESSOR

(Surprised) You know them?

LOLA

Oh, such ... style.

PROFESSOR

Such characters.

LOLA

What a writer.

PROFESSOR

A poet of the sea.

LOLA

We depend on our merchant men for ... for ... for everything they bring us!

ACT ONE

PROFESSOR

Jute, wheat, iron ore, raw cotton and crude oil. Forgive me for enquiring, Miss ... ah ...

LOLA

Lola. Just Lola.

PROFESSOR

Miss ... ah ... Lola. But you seem a lady of some background.

LOLA

Do I? Well, yes. Mine is an all too common story. The war, you know. *(Putting on her mascara.)*

PROFESSOR

(Purpling with rage) The war! Ah yes, the war, the war!

LOLA

We lost everything. *(Little spit on her mascara.)*

PROFESSOR

Never! Germany will recover! A new generation arises!

LOLA

Oh absolutely.

PROFESSOR

We shall take revenge. We shall conquer!

LOLA

I couldn't agree more.

PROFESSOR

I must confess, gnadige fraulein, I am surprised. When I discovered your name in the hands of a pupil ...

She has her leg up on the chair, fixing her stockings. RAAT is riveted by the sight of her thigh.

> PROFESSOR
> I little expected to meet a lady of such ... of such ...

> LOLA
> You were saying?

The BOYS, above him, stifle giggles.

LOLA covers by swooping on BOMBLER as he enters.

> LOLA
> Professor, may I present our dear manager, and fellow artiste, Herr Friedrich Bombler. Herr Bombler, you have the honour to meet Professor ... Professor ...

> PROFESSOR
> Raat. Professor Doktor Immanuel Raat, of the Schiller Gymnasium. *(He bows)* Senior Professor.

> BOMBLER
> Oh? O-oh! *(Bows deep)* Pleased to meet you, mein Herr. *(He shakes Raat's hand vigorously.)*

The PROFESSOR quickly pockets the silk knickers.

> BOMBLER
> So, a little reception for our lovely Lola-Lola ... art and science, art and science, eh? Very honoured, very honoured. This calls for a toast. *(Calls)* ... Mai?

> LOLA
> Perhaps a little later. *(She indicates the hiding BOYS.)*

ACT ONE

BOMBLER

What? Ah. Miss Lola is due onstage now,
Herr Professor, and you won't want to miss
her performance. *(Whispers)* we have a special table
for distinguished guests.

PROFESSOR

No, really, I ...

BOMBLER

After, you may wish to enjoy the skills of my own
humble art. *(He bows with a flourish)* Freidrich von
Bombler, prestidigitateur extraordinaire. *(He does a
trick, producing a cigarette from nowhere)* Hoop-la!
This way.

PROFESSOR

No, I ...

But LOLA smiles at him, and he allows himself to be swept away.

BOMBLER and the PROFESSOR exit.

HANS, PAUL and LUTZ emerge.

HANS

Thanks, Lola.

LUTZ

'Such characters!' 'What a writer!'

PAUL

(Murmurs to LOLA as he leaves) Such style ...

BOMBLER squires the PROFESSOR to a table, sits him down, slaps a napkin in his lap proudly, and pours champagne for him.

A DRUM ROLL.

MAI, TUMTUM and BERTHA sing the introduction to 'Beware of Blonde Women.'

LOLA makes her entrance and sings 'Beware of Blonde Women.' moving among the customers.

The PROFESSOR is enchanted. She sings to him, approaching his table and sitting on it.

Towards the end of the song LOLA, intending mischief, moves away until she reaches the BOYS' table.

The PROFESSOR sees them in the spotlight.

PROFESSOR
I see you! I see you!

He makes after them. His fury doubles as PAUL, laughing, leans to murmur something to LOLA.

PROFESSOR
Vile, corrupted youth! You are the leader, Eberhardt!
I have you at last! I see through you!

He lays about him with his umbrella.

LUTZ and HANS dodge him and make their escape.

LOLA walks away, pleased with herself as the PROFESSOR collides with BOMBLER, who reels into MAI, who is entering with champagne.

BOMBLER falls.

KLAUS lifts LOLA out of the way, and throws her to DIETER, who stands legs slightly apart, holding her with tense stillness.

MAI tries to right herself, then falls over the rising BOMBLER.

The PROFESSOR lands on top of them.

LUTZ and HANS leap over the heap and join PAUL at the exit.

ACT ONE

LOLA slides out of DIETER'S arms and laughs, throwing back her head.

Light change.

ACT ONE – SCENE FIVE.

The Professor's Lodgings. The next morning

A plain room. The table laid for breakfast. The Housekeeper, FRAU PFLUG, checks the table, muttering anxiously.

She moves the coffee pot, nods, satisfied.

FRAU PFLUG

Herr Professor! *(She steps forward.)* I've had the honour to look after Professor Raat for seventeen years. You couldn't be employed by a more regular gentleman. *(Shakes her head, puzzled.)* In all the years I've served him, I've never known the Professor to be out after midnight. *(Dismisses the thought, calls)* Herr Professor!

The PROFESSOR enters, adjusting his wing collar.

FRAU PFLUG

Guten morgen, Herr Professor.

He nods formally, checks the table, nods again and sits. He touches the side of the coffee pot.

PROFESSOR

Not hot enough! Again, I must complain.

She lifts the pot, wincing at its heat.

PROFESSOR

And while we are on the subject of my domestic
arrangements, I must amend my instructions
on the laundering of my collars. Delete the order
'stiffly starched.' Replace with the order 'very
stiffly starched. A man in my position, Frau Pflug,
cannot appear before pupils and staff at the Schiller
Gymnasium with inadequately starched collars. Oh,
put it down!

He mops his head with his handkerchief. But finds LOLA's knickers in his hand. He drops them on the table, aghast.

FRAU PFLUG

(*Bleats faintly*) Herr Professor ... ?

She waves the coffee pot in agitation. The knickers are on the only clear spot. There is no room for the coffee pot.

PROFESSOR

Remove that insolence!

FRAU PFLUG leans over the table.

PROFESSOR

Wait! Give them – it – to me. (*He picks up the
knickers with an attempt at insouciance.*) Whoever
is responsible for this practical joke will be punished
accordingly.

But FRAU PFLUG makes the mistake of stifling a giggle behind her hand. And gets a cold glare.

PROFESSOR

That is what comes of allowing the children of
tradesmen into the Gymnasium.

ACT ONE

FRAU PFLUG

(Faint) Yes, Herr Professor.

She stands before him humbly as he drinks coffee and crunches a sugar bun.

PROFESSOR

So kindly do not continue to mention your nephew to me, Frau Pflug.

The CLOCK STRIKES. He rises, holds out his arms. FRAU PFLUG helps him on with his cloak, and gives him his cane.

She clears her throat.

FRAU PFLUG

Herr Professor ... your hat ... *(She clears her throat again)* ... your hat ...

He glares at her.

FRAU PFLUG

(Swallowing) It appears that your hat is not here, Herr Professor. Your hat is not in its accustomed place. I do not see your hat at all, anywhere!

PROFESSOR

Indeed. And are you suggesting that it has been stolen from the premises?

FRAU PFLUG

Herr Professor! It is possible ... you were out at an engagement last night. Could it be that ... that ...

PROFESSOR

You will not refer to my personal affairs. Whether I am in or out is not a matter for gossip below stairs. If my hat left the house with me, then my hat ... *(But he suddenly remembers. He has left his hat at The Blue Angel.)* Be so good as to fetch my top hat.

FRAU PFLUG
(She is astonished.) Your ... you ...

PROFESSOR
Do as I say, woman!

She flies out in terror, and returns, brushing at his top hat wildly with a brush. He snatches it and clamps it on his head.

PROFESSOR
Thoroughly unsatisfactory. You will be hearing from me further.

He exits.

FRAU PFLUG
(Looks after him.) You miserable old ... ! He never misses a chance. *TWO* pots of coffee, and will *he* pay for the extra starch? No fear! I'd like to grind you in the grinder, you old Blucher.

Light change.

ACT ONE - SCENE SIX.

On the Street.

HANS, PAUL and LUTZ.

They kick a strapped bundle of PAUL's sports shirt and gym shoes between them, skillfully heel-kicking it up.

LUTZ dives for the bundle and they mob him. There is a brief tussle. They sprawl on the ground, getting their breath back.

ACT ONE

LUTZ

(Groans loudly) I can't bear the suspense!

HANS

He's not going to do anything.

PAUL

The man's ignored us all day.

LUTZ

He's playing with us. Oh Christ.

HANS

What?

LUTZ

He's going to fail us.

PAUL

After what we saw last night?

HANS

(Dramatic, with gestures.) Revenge!

LUTZ

All right for you. Your father has pull. What is it, one of Germany's Big Five Industrialists?

PAUL

Stop worrying.

LUTZ

... and yours is a Junker. Ja, ja, Herr Baron ... nein, nein Herr Baron ... *(He groans comically.)* Mine's a coal merchant. *(He does a cringing walk, clutching his coat lapels together.)* The Scapegoat. *(He flops down, head on his elbow.)*

They lie back, relaxing.

HANS

God, she makes your balls ache.

LUTZ thumps him.

HANS

Ow!

LUTZ

I've told you, don't talk about her like that! I can't stop thinking about her. I'd ask her to marry me if I didn't know she'd laugh in my face.

PAUL

Don't be a fool.

LUTZ

Oh, we know where you stand. The right alliance. An heir and a spare – and *then* fornication.

HANS

Why not?

PAUL

Grow up, Lutz. Lola's for pleasure. Take what you can and forget about her. Anything else ... For God's sake – if you were ever stupid enough to marry a girl like that, you'd find yourself out of a job, out of money, out of respect – out of everything.

LUTZ

It's easy for you to talk. I don't know what to do. Some nights I think ... I think, if I can't have her ... if she won't – I might as well do myself in.

PAUL

Don't be a fool!

ACT ONE

HANS

Forget her. Worry about your exams.

LUTZ groans loudly.

LUTZ

He'll fail me, I know it. I shall end up in military school, the prey of some filthy nonce with hairs in his nose.

PAUL shakes his head.

PAUL

Sewer won't do anything.

HANS gets up.

HANS

He has something on us.

PAUL

We have something on him.

HANS

Impasse!

HANS makes fencing passes. PAUL jumps up, and he and HANS circle each other, fencing style, making passes. PAUL stops.

PAUL

I know. We'll go to Lola's.

LUTZ

What?!

PAUL

The safest place in Hamburg.

HANS

You're right! *(He bounds off, turns, jogging backwards.)* Don't worry about the Sewer-Raat. He'll be lying low tonight!

PAUL hauls LUTZ to his feet. They go, laughing.

Light change.

ACT ONE – SCENE SEVEN.

The Blue Angel.

The sound of MUSIC offstage.

DIETER enters. Alone, he picks up LOLA's dressing gown, presses it to his face, inhaling her scent. He drops it hurriedly and goes as ...

BOMBLER enters, fondling the CLUB WAITRESS.

MAI
(Offstage, calls) Fred!

BOMBLER and the WAITRESS go quickly.

MAI enters.

MAI

Fred! Where is he, the devil? The house is open!

KLAUS, in a new costume with leopard skin, tries his weights as TUMTUM and BERTHA sit in the dressing area. They take out a huge sausage, and pare off slices, and eat.

HERMINE, apart, curls her hair with tongs and listens in.

Enter LOLA.

ACT ONE

KLAUS

(To LOLA, turning to show off his new costume.)
Well?

LOLA

Sensational.

KLAUS preens.

LOLA

Found the python?

KLAUS

Nah. He'll turn up.

TUMTUM

More fleisch, Bertha?

BERTHA

Just a touch.

TUMTUM hacks off half the sausage, and gives it to her.

LOLA

So. Any progress?

The GIRLS shake their heads.

TUMTUM

Still just sits there.

LOLA

No sign of a ring?

HERMINE

He did buy her some shoe polish.

BERTHA nods, smiling.

LOLA

Oh good. I should put up the banns.

TUMTUM

(Sighs) It must be nice to be in love. Did you ever do it because you wanted to, Lola?

LOLA

Hullo, what's all this? Tumtum, have you been courting?

She tickles TUMTUM, making her squeak.

TUMTUM

Pax. Pax! I only wondered if you'd ever been in love!

LOLA

Love? Me? *(Laughs)* You don't want to believe all that rubbish. Ruin your life, that will. Oh no, none of that.

KLAUS

Visitors.

He lets in HANS, LUTZ and PAUL.

BERTHA

Oh, not the ruddy nursery again.

Both TUMTUM and HERMINE attack her physically.

HERMINE leers at HANS, who takes no notice.

LOLA

Come in!

HANS

Lola. For you. *(He presents her with a large box of chocolates.)*

LOLA

You darlings!

TUMTUM

Montelimar!

ACT ONE

BERTHA

Truffles!

The GIRLS fall on the chocolates, quarrelling.

TUMTUM

I only like the soft ones ... Hey, you've had two!

LOLA rescues the box. HANS and LUTZ take chocolates eagerly, making LOLA laugh. She offers the box to PAUL. He shakes his head.

LOLA

(To PAUL) How's Professor Raat?

But PAUL turns away.

LOLA

(Addressing HANS.) Any trouble?

HANS

No!

She laughs, and holds out the bottom of her skirt for LUTZ to hold as she darns it. He kneels before her. PAUL smiles faintly.

LOLA

Not every night I entertain a Professor. *(She bites off the cotton with her teeth, bending over LUTZ.)*

HANS

He won't put his nose in here again.

LUTZ

Not the old Sewer Rat.

HERMINE

Sewer Rat?

TUMTUM

Ugh!

BERTHA

What do you call him that for?

LUTZ

Because he's loathsome.

HANS

Evil.

LUTZ

Monster.

HANS chases TUMTUM, scuttling after her. She squeals.

LUTZ

He treats us as if it's our fault.

LOLA

What?

LUTZ

(Shrugs helplessly) Don't know. Everything.

LOLA frowns, puzzled, at PAUL.

PAUL

Germany losing the war. The Wagnerian dream shattered.

TUMTUM

Well, that's not your fault.

HANS

He hates us.

HERMINE

What for?

HANS

(Closing on her) Because we're so vital and handsome!

ACT ONE

LUTZ

(Lifting TUMTUM) And strong!

HANS and LUTZ grab BERTHA and TUMTUM, making them yell. HERMINE beats them off scornfully, protecting her dress.

KLAUS

Customers, girls!

MAI

Come on, come on! We've got members of the paying public out there.

BERTHA and TUMTUM hurtle onstage to perform.

HANS and LUTZ follow, to watch.

LOLA

(To PAUL) Perhaps you shouldn't stay.

They stand together, close.

LOLA

He could be back.

PAUL

(Close) He won't come here again.

LOLA

Are you sure?

LOLA exits.

PAUL follows.

BERTHA and TUMTUM and KLAUS perform '*Wenn die Beste Freundin.*'

The PROFESSOR enters the empty dressing room.

He pauses, looks around, decides to leave, but pauses at her dressing table for a look. He picks up a photograph of her, and studies it closely.

The SONG FINISHES.

LOLA enters, and watches him.

> LOLA
> (*Softly*) We-ell. So, you've come to see me.

> PROFESSOR
> (*Jumps*) I beg your pardon. I am sorry to intrude.

> LOLA
> Sit down, Herr Professor. Please. Why shouldn't you come back? I'm very honoured. And just in time to do your homework.

She proffers her make-up tray. This time he takes it willingly.

It is already a ritual.

He pulls up a chair and holds the hand-mirror for her.

> LOLA
> Closer ... closer. There. Very still. I forbid you to move. (*Putting on mascara*) You're much nicer today.

She waves him to move the hand-mirror so she can see.

He concentrates meticulously on getting the right angle for her.

She finishes, and blows powder in his face. He jumps, and then laughs, very excited.

> LOLA
> Thank you for coming. We artistes depend so much on appreciation. It's our food, our drink. We breathe it in, like the scent of flowers. After all, what are we

but butterflies, Herr Professor? We live so briefly ...
so briefly.

PROFESSOR

You have a poetic mind, Miss Lola. Enchanting.
Enchanting.

LOLA

The pleasure is mine. To talk to a man of education ...
style ...

She puts a hand on his arm, wheels him as she sees the BOYS approaching. She waves them back.

LOLA

So kind of you to call. I am very flattered.

PROFESSOR

(Embarrassed) Oh well, I have to confess, gnadige
Fraulein, that I ... there is a reason for my brief
entrée. My hat.

LOLA

Your hat?

PROFESSOR

My hat. Unfortunately, in my natural haste yesterday
to apprehend the miscreants who ... who were
making a nuisance of themselves ...

LOLA

Dear, dear Herr Professor. Please forgive them. Their
natural desire not to lose your esteem ... They lost
their heads. Of course, they were at fault. *(She shakes her head soberly)* Gravely ...

PROFESSOR

And you may rest assured, for your sake, they will be punished ...

LOLA assumes a tragic aspect.

LOLA

Never! How could I come between a revered and honoured man such as yourself, and your charges! They are your life. Yours to lead, yours to restrain, yours to encourage. As for me, I am nothing. Think of me only as a poor ... *(She searches for a word somewhat desperately)* ... hummingbird ... who brushed your cheek for a brief moment.

She brushes her hand lightly down his cheek.

He is so overcome, he drops her make-up. They grope for it together. He takes her hand to kiss it.

LOLA

Promise me, dear Professor, that you will forgive your boys. Give them, as you always have, the guidance of an experienced, authoritative man. *(She puts a finger on his mouth)* Our lips are sealed. Secrets.

They almost kiss but she breaks it up briskly, seeing she has won.

He compromises by kissing her hand.

And jumps as BOMBLER, finishing his tricks to a DRUM ROLL AND APPLAUSE, enters.

Followed by KLAUS.

BOMBLER

I ask for a dove, and he gives me a sausage! Herr Professor! Again, an honour!

ACT ONE

PROFESSOR

(Stiff bow) Mein Herr.

BOMBLER

Delighted to receive you. Champagne! Champagne for the Professor!

PROFESSOR

No, no. I regret – no, no ...

BOMBLER

Not at all, my dear sir. I assure you the honour is all ours. Klaus, the keys to the cellar!

KLAUS

What?

BOMBLER waves him off irritably.

BOMBLER

I shall arrange your seat as before. Incognito, eh? In-cognito?

He bustles off.

LOLA

You will stay for my performance?

PROFESSOR

I regret, impossible. I think ... ah ... just the hat.

LOLA

Oh, the hat. *(Screeches, forgetting to be Camille for the moment)* Anyone seen the Professor's hat? What 'ave you done with his hat?!

DIETER enters silently, proffers the hat, then clowns with it up his arm. The PROFESSOR accepts it with a curt nod.

KLAUS enters with champagne, and wheels away without stopping as the PROFESSOR waves him off.

LOLA and he are alone. He waves his hat apologetically.

Then remembers.

> PROFESSOR
>
> Ah. I was forgetting.

He takes out the knickers, now wrapped in brown paper and tied with string.

> LOLA
>
> (*Thinking it is a present.*) For me? But how kind!

> PROFESSOR
>
> No. Ah ... I ... I ... your ... I took them in mistake for my hat – ah ... handkerchief!

> LOLA
>
> Oh ... yes. (*Opening the parcel*) Professor! So this wasn't a social call after all! (*She pulls a sad face.*)

> PROFESSOR
>
> I would not distress you for all the world, believe me.

> LOLA
>
> I'm disappointed.

> PROFESSOR
>
> Nothing in the world would make me happier than to ...

BOMBLER enters, shoving KLAUS out of the way.

> BOMBLER
>
> All is arranged, mein Herr. The special table ...

> KLAUS
>
> He said he didn't want it!

ACT ONE

BOMBLER kicks KLAUS.

>   BOMBLER
>
> Your champagne awaits you. I took the liberty of
> leaving a plate of sauerkraut. One must look after the
> inner man, nicht wahr? Ha ha!

There is a moment of indecision. LOLA lifts her knickers and holds them tenderly in her hands. He is lost.

>   LOLA
>
> Please ...

He beams, dazzled.

KLAUS and BOMBLER squire him away firmly.

HANS and LUTZ creep in.

>   LOLA
>
> You, out!

They go, laughing. LOLA is ruminative. She walks about thoughtfully.

>   LOLA
>
> There must be a pfennig in it somewhere.

The MUSICAL INTRODUCTION.

LOLA, side-stage, clenches and unclenches her hands, nervous. She makes her entrance.

She sings 'Falling in Love Again.'

In the middle of the song, a Dutch CAPTAIN tries to grab her. She handles him easily, smiling in friendly fashion.

>   CAPTAIN
>
> A drink! A drink with you, Lola-Lola ...

The PROFESSOR rushes up.

PROFESSOR
Take your hands off that lady.

CAPTAIN
Lola! Are you going to help me spend the insurance?
My ship went down!

PROFESSOR
Take your hands off, sir ... I insist!

CAPTAIN
We'll drink to Lloyds together, eh?

PROFESSOR
Out sir! Out! This lady does not drink with anyone.
She has no interest in your affairs!

CAPTAIN
Who's the old fool? Get off!

The CAPTAIN jabs the PROFESSOR heavily in the stomach with his elbow. The PROFESSOR staggers, and becomes totally enraged. He attacks the CAPTAIN.

The two aging, heavily-built men grapple, both puffing.

TUMTUM
(Shrieks) Quick, somebody, help! Call the police!

BOMBLER
(Cuffs her) Shut up, you fool!

The call is taken up. 'Police! Police!'

The two MEN roll over and over. KLAUS and BOMBLER try to separate them. BERTHA clouts everyone within reach.

TUMTUM
That's it, Bertha!

ACT ONE

MAI

Mind the glasses!

BERTHA

(Calls to LOLA) A real professor! You're going up in the world!

BERTHA butts the CAPTAIN in the stomach cheerfully.

A POLICEMAN enters. There is silence at once.

The PROFESSOR struggles to his feet. And to his senses. He is appalled by what has happened.

CAPTAIN

This ole' fool started it. He was on me before even I saw 'im. I didn't stand a chance.

POLICEMAN

Name?

CAPTAIN

Captain van Outen, of the Marindora. I came to renew an old acquaintance with the lady and, before I was through the door ...

POLICEMAN

(To the PROFESSOR.) Name?

PROFESSOR

I am Professor Immanuel Raat, of the Schiller Gymnasium.

The POLICEMAN's manner alters at once. He stands to attention.

POLICEMAN

Herr Professor. *(He gives a slight bow)* You wish to make a complaint against this man?

PROFESSOR

I do indeed. I am here on official business followinginformation that some of my pupils were frequenting this ... this establishment. I was forced, as a gentleman, to intervene, when this pig of a foreigner made an offence of himself towards the lady. In the first place, he is intoxicated ...

POLICEMAN

Right, sir. *(To the CAPTAIN)* Come along with me.

CAPTAIN

(Crestfallen) How was I to know he was a Professor?

POLICEMAN

(To BOMBLER, accepting a bribe) You'd better shut up shop. We don't want any trouble.

CAPTAIN

He was standing up for the whore! What's it got to do with him? Why doesn't he stick to his school? You can't go anywhere these days ...

The CAPTAIN exits, followed by the POLICEMAN.

BOMBLER

Right, we'll pack it in for the night.

MAI

The hell we will.

BOMBLER

(Showing her his fist) Shut your face.

MAI, furious, stomps off.

PAUL picks up the PROFESSOR'S hat, dusts it, and hands it to him.

The PROFESSOR blenches when he sees who it is.

ACT ONE

PAUL

(Quietly) Your hat, Professor.

PROFESSOR

Oh yes. I see through you. How dare you defy me? How dare you come back here?

PAUL

I am here for the reason you are here.

PROFESSOR

And what do you mean by that?

He glares at PAUL. Who looks steadily back.

PAUL

I don't think there's any more to be said.

PROFESSOR

You don't ... You don't think ... ?

But PAUL turns to leave. The PROFESSOR calls.

PROFESSOR

She does not want you here! Any of you! But particularly you!

PAUL turns, glances at him, and goes.

PROFESSOR

(Calls) She has someone to protect her now!

Only LOLA and the PROFESSOR are left.

He collapses onto a chair as BOMBLER re-enters to lock up and switch off the lights.

LOLA

Are you all right, Herr Professor?

PROFESSOR

I am not used to this.

LOLA

No, I don't suppose you are.

She finds him a drink.

BOMBLER turns off the main light.

LOLA

Here. Brandy.

PROFESSOR

Thank you.

He takes the glass doubtfully, and drinks. She looks down at his ruffled hair and disordered necktie.

LOLA

Better?

She clicks her fingers behind her.

BOMBLER drops the keys into her palm, turns off another light, and goes.

PROFESSOR

I believe so.

He cannot take his eyes from her. He gazes up at her face, then makes a sudden lunge, grasps her hand feverishly and crushes it to his middle like a determined child.

LOLA

(Gently) Like that, is it?

PROFESSOR

I cannot stop looking at you.

ACT ONE

LOLA

Get up. *(He gazes at her, then rises obediently.)* Come.

They climb the stairs to her boudoir.

He sits on the bed. She begins to undress him.

PROFESSOR

No ... please ... please ...

But she is masterful. And puts a hand on him.

LOLA

What have we here?

PROFESSOR

No, please ... no ... oh ... ohh!

LOLA

I think we have a naughty boy here ...

PROFESSOR

No ... *(He gives a strange, high cry and leaps on her.)* You ... You are the wicked one. You ... you ... you!

ACT ONE - SCENE EIGHT.

The Schoolroom.

The school BELL rings.

LUTZ and HANS are drawing an obscene picture of LOLA and the PROFESSOR on the blackboard.

HANS

Put the titties in! And the other bit. Go on!

The PROFESSOR enters, formal and glowering.

He goes to his desk, puts down his register, turns and sees the drawing.

                PROFESSOR
(*Turning ferociously*) Who is responsible for this?

The BOYS begin to whisper: 'Lola, Lola,' gradually getting louder and louder.

Then another group chants 'Sewer Rat, Sewer Rat.'

HANS conducts them. Cacophony.

The HEADMASTER enters.

Silence. The BOYS sit up straight, arms folded.

                HEADMASTER
Should this class not be in the science laboratory for the next session?

                PROFESSOR
That is correct.

                HEADMASTER
Be kind enough to give the order.

                PROFESSOR
(*Clears his throat*) Proceed in double file to Science Laboratory Four. No speaking in the corridors.

The BOYS leave.

The HEADMASTER approaches the board, and regards it gravely

                HEADMASTER
(*Quietly*) Professor Raat. There is a matter, I think, that you may wish to discuss with me.

ACT ONE

PROFESSOR

The perpetrators of this obscenity will be severely punished.

HEADMASTER

Alas, I am afraid that the situation has gone beyond the confines of this classroom.

PROFESSOR

Pray what do you mean? You cannot, surely, be influenced by the slanders of disobedient and recalcitrant students? I demand names!

HEADMASTER

You are mistaken. None of your students has spoken. There is, however, a good deal of gossip in the town.

PROFESSOR

I have no intention of listening to calumny. I am surprised, Herr Headmaster, that you are not more protective of a long-established member of your staff. May I remind you that I have given twenty-five years to this college.

HEADMASTER

Believe me, I find the matter very painful ... very distressing. *(He walks, turns)* How can you risk your reputation for such a woman? You are a bachelor. Your private life is your own affair – to some extent. But to go off the rails. To behave so wildly, over such a ... I'm sorry, but I must speak plainly ...

PROFESSOR

(Interrupts) Headmaster, I insist. *(He lifts a hand)* I must forbid you to talk in this manner of my future wife.

HEADMASTER

(*Very startled*) Wife? You cannot be serious!

PROFESSOR

I intend to offer the young lady my hand. Under the circumstances, you will understand that this conversation must cease forthwith.

HEADMASTER

(*Flabbergasted*) Raat, my dear fellow! Consider what you are doing! You cannot seriously be thinking of casting aside a life's work? You are a pillar of this institution. Your conduct has always been utterly beyond reproach!

PROFESSOR

It is my privilege to marry whom I choose. The lady who does me the honour to take my name will, I trust, thereby be offered the protection of my status.

Silence. The HEADMASTER shakes his head.

HEADMASTER

May I ask ... does the young ... the young ... ah ... lady know of your intentions towards her?

PROFESSOR

I have no doubt that she returns my regard.

HEADMASTER

But you haven't made her a formal offer?

PROFESSOR

(*Shakes his head*) No.

HEADMASTER

Then please, I ask you, pause. Reflect. These are restless times, Herr Professor. Men such as yourself

ACT ONE

are vital to the rehabilitation of Germany. I cannot afford to let you go. Let me arrange a sabbatical. (*His voice softens*) Immanuel! We are old colleagues – more – old comrades in arms! We stand together.

PROFESSOR

(*After a long pause*) I'm sorry. I cannot be shaken from my intention to ask the lady to do me the honour of becoming my wife.

HEADMASTER

That ... is very sad.

Silence. The HEADMASTER moves slowly to the door.

HEADMASTER

You realise what this means?

PROFESSOR

I have no doubt, sir, that my experience as a schoolmaster will be acceptable in some other district. It is possible to be too long in one place. In any case, I could not agree to remain in a situation where my wife was not received with the deference due to her as my consort.

The HEADMASTER, at the door, gives him a long, sad look.

The PROFESSOR looks at him.

PROFESSOR

I may depend upon you for a reference?

HEADMASTER

You must know that is out of the question.

PROFESSOR

No reference?

HEADMASTER

Quite impossible. My dear Immanuel, if you marry this woman...

PROFESSOR

But it's within my power to save the soul of another human being! Otto, we are Christian men! Have you forgotten the Magdalene?

HEADMASTER

I'm sorry.

PROFESSOR

But...

HEADMASTER

My dear Raat, there must be rules.

He leaves, with a last glance at the PROFESSOR.

Alone, the PROFESSOR sits heavily.

LUTZ, HANS and PAUL enter.

PROFESSOR

What do you want?

LUTZ

I have to give out the prep, sir.

PROFESSOR

No.

LUTZ stops in his tracks.

PROFESSOR

There will be no preparation tonight.

LUTZ

(*Puzzled*) No prep?

ACT ONE

PROFESSOR

Out!

HANS

Sir ... sir! We have to have our prep.

But under his glower the BOYS exit, confused.

After a still moment to recover himself, the PROFESSOR looks up and around the empty schoolroom. He opens his class register.

PROFESSOR

(Reads) ... Ehrmann ... Eisendorf ... Kohl ... Markowsky ... Schelling ... Schmidt ... Tauber ... von Eberhardt.

The JANITOR stands by the door.

PROFESSOR

(Before seeing who it is) What is it?

JANITOR

It's Steufnagel, sir.

PROFESSOR

Very well, carry on. Clean the blackboard.

The JANITOR picks up his bucket and mop, and advances. He has an appalling limp. He sees the blackboard and makes a sound of shock. He quickly wipes the board.

JANITOR

(Low) Herr Professor ... (He seems broken) Is it true?

The PROFESSOR turns.

PROFESSOR

That I am leaving the school? Yes, it is true.

JANITOR

But ... Please, sir! You are our stanchion! (*He shuffles forward like a spider.*) The departments won't function, sir. Not without you. You are the right-hand man here!

The PROFESSOR contemplates him. He puts out a hand, almost but not quite touching STEUFNAGEL.

PROFESSOR

Go home, Steufnagel. You have my permission.

The JANITOR pauses, then, with his bucket and mop, he limps sadly away.

The PROFESSOR sits.

He rises, takes his books under one arm, and, carrying his briefcase, and goes, with an almost eager step.

Light change.

ACT ONE – SCENE NINE.

The Blue Angel.

Baskets and trunks onstage.

The TROUPE are rehearsing a new act – an Apache dance.

KLAUS lifts HERMINE high. She wobbles.

BERTHA and TUMTUM watch.

A PIANIST and DIETER accompany them.

MAI and BOMBLER stop rehearsing. The rest continue.

ACT ONE

BOMBLER

(He waves a paper under her nose.) Eighteen bottles of gin?

MAI

I need it! What about *her*? All the champagne!

BOMBLER

She brings the Professor in. Raises the tone.

MAI

(Sarcastic) Oh, well!

The rehearsal continues.

MAI

(Grumbles) I'm not standing for it. I could get you for interfering with your niece. That's illegal. And what about Stuttgart?

BOMBLER

Shut up. All right, call it off, time to pack ...

They don't hear him.

MAI

Begrudging me a drop! *I'm* an artiste, too, you know.

BOMBLER

Can't I get it into your Neanderthal skull? *(speaking under MAI'S lines)* I swear I'll swing for her! We're skint! I'm cleaned out paying doctors' bills. What with his *(points to KLAUS)* – her ... *(points to HERMINE.)*

HERMINE, wobbling, is perching on KLAUS's shoulders.

KLAUS

(To BERTHA) How does it look?

BERTHA

The same.

TUMTUM

Worse.

BERTHA

(Eating) Smile, Hermine!

TUMTUM

(Eating) She's too deadpan.

BOMBLER

Call it off, you two. Start packing!

KLAUS and HERMINE stop rehearsing.

BOMBLER

(He turns on MAI.) It cost me a fortune for Lola's bit of trouble.

MAI

If Lola got knocked up, she should have paid her own bill. It's nothing to do with you.

BOMBLER looks sheepish. The others exchange looks.

MAI

Oh. Oh, I see. *(She collapses, crying.)*

HERMINE

Leave Mutti alone.

BOMBLER

And you stay out of it. Make yourself useful.

HERMINE

Daddy!

ACT ONE

BOMBLER

Urrgh! If the Titanic were sailing tomorrow I'd book 'em both first class tickets. Pay for your own gin – I'm not coughing up.

BOMBLER exits.

MAI

Beast! You tell him to keep his hands off you, Tumtum. I'll write to your mother if he doesn't watch out. Don't worry, I'll see he leaves you alone.

TUMTUM

I don't mind, really.

MAI gives her a black look.

LOLA enters, dazzling in street clothes.

MAI

(Sour) Oh, talk of the devil!

LOLA

(Quick on the uptake) What's up?

HERMINE

You should know.

MAI

I hear you've been costing us again. I can't even get the price of a bottle of gin!

LOLA

Mai – don't listen. He only does it for spite.

MAI

I'm fed up with him. What's that?

LOLA

(She has a wrapped bottle.) Schnapps. For the journey. *(But she unwraps it.)*

BOMBLER enters at the back, carrying a small skip.

LOLA

Here.

She gives MAI some schnapps. MAI settles.

TUMTUM

Any cake?

TUMTUM and BERTHA dive into the bag. BOMBLER throws down the skip and goes.

LOLA

What's he been saying?

MAI

(Sour) It's all right for you.

DIETER brings in a packing case.

MAI

Make yourself useful, you girls.

TUMTUM and BERTHA pick up cases and exit.

MAI

Not you, Hermine, you're too dainty. Go and fold your undies.

HERMINE moves off reluctantly.

MAI

I'm the one supposed to be his wife!

BERTHA, TUMTUM and KLAUS move skips across the stage.

ACT ONE

LOLA

Yes, but you don't like him. Every time he tries anything, you yell blue murder.

MAI

Of course I do! He's horrible.

LOLA

Well, then. Somebody has to keep him sweet.

BERTHA, KLAUS and TUMTUM exit.

LOLA

If it's any consolation, I don't enjoy it.

MAI

What do you do it for then?

LOLA

He's the Guvnor! You have to keep in.

MAI, irritated, grabs the bottle of schnapps.

MAI

He wasn't always so horrible! P'raps he was. *(She is becoming mellow with the drink.)*

LOLA

Don't see why I should come in for it. I ought to be thinking about my future, making plans, I don't want to end up like you. Oh, sorry.

LOLA refills her glass.

MAI

That's all right. I should have pushed off before me looks went. *(She becomes tearful.)* It doesn't last forever. You've hardly got it before it's gone. And when you've got it, you haven't got enough of it.

LOLA nods in sympathy.

                    MAI

All right for you.

                    LOLA

Think so?

She helps herself to a drink. They both drink, put down their glasses and light up.

                    LOLA

(*Sighs deeply*) What I need is a nice old geezer to come through that door, and whisk me off to the Riviera in his Mercedes-Benz.

                    MAI

Me too.

                    LOLA

That'd be the life. Shove him off to business, breakfast in bed, maid to run the bath. Off out shopping ...

                    MAI

Whee!

                    LOLA

... lunch with a friend ...

                    MAI

Male or female?

                    LOLA

All the same to me! (*They laugh, screeching together.*) Touch of mischief in the afternoon. Look in the nursery at five. Little boy, little girl. Change for dinner. Off to the theatre. Watch fools like us slogging it out. Smoked salmon supper. Posh nightclub. Ohh, what a life!

ACT ONE

MAI

You'd never get out of bed.

LOLA

To spend his cash, I would. He'd get his money's worth. I'd be better than most of the frigid bitches they end up with. I'd be a good bargain.

MAI

I know you would.

LOLA

I'm wasted here.

MAI

Well, stop dreaming. It'll never happen.

A knock on the door.

MAI

(*She yells*) What do you want?

The PROFESSOR enters. He carries a large bunch of flowers.

MAI

No school, Professor?

MAI staggers off discreetly.

LOLA

Professor. How sweet of you to come and bid us farewell. For me? How charming. Truly charming.

PROFESSOR

Miss Lola...

LOLA

I've enjoyed your visits. Who knows? Perhaps we shall meet again someday?

PROFESSOR

I don't wish you to go.

Outside the door, MAI listens.

LOLA

Alas! When one is penniless it is necessary to earn a living, however humbly.

PROFESSOR

I wish you to stay.

LOLA

I wish I could, too. Never mind, we'll be back in the summer, after the tour.

PROFESSOR

Marry me! Marry me, dearest Miss Lola! Then we need never be parted.

MAI reacts in amazement.

LOLA

What?! *(She bursts out laughing.)*

PROFESSOR

You find it amusing. I am sorry. No. I am pleased to amuse you. No doubt you find my offer ridiculous?

LOLA

No ... no, no! Dear Professor, not at all, but you can't be serious!

PROFESSOR

I am completely serious. *(He goes on his knees, formally and carefully.)* Miss Lola. You cannot be unaware of my growing attachment to you. Indeed, I have been bold enough to hope that you returned at least some of my affection. You have *(stumbles)* ...

received me here at night ... we ... we ... I have been in heaven ... in heaven! *(He grasps her knees)* I cannot do without you. I crave for you night and day! I never believed that such bliss could exist. For the first time in my life, I am alive!

LOLA

(Frees herself gently.) Yes, I know. You've been quite a jolly boy.

PROFESSOR

I come to you with my heart whole. There have been ... when I was younger ... there were ladies who ... with whom I might have formed an alliance. But I was too shy. They were women of my own class, and it did not seem possible to approach them.

LOLA

Sure. That's what women like me are for.

PROFESSOR

I will raise you up. With the protection of my name you can begin a new life. I forgive the sordid nature of your past. We will move away, to another city. Wipe the slate clean.

He becomes courageous and envelopes LOLA in a fervent, clumsy embrace.

MAI, at the door, prevents BOMBLER from entering.

MAI

Stay out, you fool! He's asking her to marry him!

BOMBLER

Good God! *(He peeps through the door.)*

MAI

She can get him for breach of promise. I'm a witness!

BOMBLER

Who's going to believe you? Get out the way!

MAI

Don't! *(She tries to restrain him from going in.)*

BOMBLER

We can't afford to lose Lola. We'd never get a replacement. I'm not getting left with you, you cow.

They glare at each other.

Then MAI, full of rage at him, bursts in, screaming with delight at the sight of the PROFESSOR and LOLA embracing.

MAI

Oh, my dear children! Does this mean? Oh, Fred, look at the dear lovebirds! Professor, are we to congratulate you?

PROFESSOR

Oh, I do hope so, my dear lady. I do hope so. Herr Bombler, it grieves me to tell you that I may be about to steal away your star performer!

BOMBLER

What's this about, Lolie?

LOLA shrugs. She helps herself to a quick schnapps.

BOMBLER

Herr Professor. Perhaps, as men of the world, a little discussion over a glass of wine? You have your position to consider. Our modest troupe must not be the cause of a disruption to your standing in society.

ACT ONE

PROFESSOR

Herr Bombler. I am offering the lady the protection of my name.

MAI

She'll be a lady, you fool! She'll have a Dresden dinner service! A wine merchant, a maid! Go on, Lola, don't dwell, take your chance, girl, you might not get another!

PROFESSOR

If I may say so, very wise counsel.

MAI

(Transported) A motor car! Could you – could you run to a motor car, Herr Professor?

PROFESSOR

Why not? Why not?

BOMBLER

(Apart) Bloody fool. *(To LOLA)* Use your head. There won't be any maids or motor cars. If he marries you, he's finished. He'll lose his place. Marry a whore and get away with it?

PROFESSOR

I must ask you for an immediate apology for those words. Otherwise I shall be forced to call you out, sir.

BOMBLER

Lola – be your age!

LOLA moves prudently between them.

LOLA

(To the PROFESSOR.) He's right. You can't marry me. You'll be ruined.

PROFESSOR

I don't care!

BOMBLER

But she does. Take my word for it. She does.

PROFESSOR

I will protect you. As a man of the world I ...

BOMBLER

Man of the world? If you were, you'd ...

MAI

Will you shut up!

BOMBLER

Lola, make him see sense!

KLAUS, HERMINE, BERTHA and TUMTUM come in.

HERMINE

What's up? I can't see.

BERTHA

It's Lola ...

MAI

Do it!

PROFESSOR

We will begin a new life together.

LOLA

Where?

PROFESSOR

Another city where together we can make a new start. As the wife of Professor Immanuel Raat you will be sans reproche.

ACT ONE

BERTHA

Wife?

TUMTUM

Oooh ... go on, Lola!

The TROUPE urge her on.

PROFESSOR

(Calls above the noise) Beloved Lola, give me your answer.

Silence. They all wait.

LOLA

All right then. Yes!

ACT ONE - SCENE TEN.

On the Street. Night.

PAUL walks up and down. He peers anxiously down the street.

He stops, tries to contain himself. He lights a cigarette, cupping his hands, and resumes walking, stamping against the cold. He calls, to the stars.

PAUL

Lola! *(And stops himself abruptly as, craning, he sees her. He waits 'casually' as she enters. Indifferently)* Oh, there you are.

LOLA

Have you been waiting?

PAUL

No. *(He closes on her.)* Is it true?

She looks at him and moves away.

PAUL

It *is* true. You can't. It's obscene.

He comes closer to her.

PAUL

I thought they were joking.

She takes his cigarette, draws on it, gives it back. Laughs.

LOLA

I've a feeling a sense of humour could do for both of us, you and me.

PAUL

You mean it's a joke?

He groans, shakes her gently.

PAUL

Tell me it's you in your devilish mood ... having us on. A marvellous revenge ...

LOLA

Revenge? For what? He's done me no harm. He's asked me to marry him. For all your looks, your poetry, you want everything for nothing.

PAUL

Listen, Lola. Respectability is not ... You'll pay a high price, believe me. You probably won't achieve it anyway.

LOLA

Who cares?

PAUL

Then what? Why?

ACT ONE

LOLA

Nothing, Herr Baron. You couldn't possibly understand.

He takes her in his arms. For a second she resists. Then she looks up at him, her face pale.

LOLA

I'm tired.

He enfolds her tenderly. They kiss.

Light change.

ACT ONE – SCENE ELEVEN.

The Wedding Party.

BOMBLER, MAI, TUMTUM, BERTHA, KLAUS, DIETER, HERMINE and the WAITRESS enter. KLAUS holds out the chairs for the BRIDE and GROOM.

BOMBLER

(Rises) A toast! A toast, meine Damen und Herren, to the happy couple!

He and KLAUS pour drinks and glasses are raised.

BOMBLER

To Frau and Professor Raat!

ALL

Frau and Professor Raat!

DIETER leaves, knocking over his chair.

A second's silence, then laughter and cheers.

The BAND strikes up '*Auf Wiedersehn.*'

>   BOMBLER
> (*Announces*) ... Damen und Herren ... it's always
> sad when we have to leave the Blue Angel. No, no. We
> feel Hamburg is our home. We'll be here again in six
> months to entertain you. However, however ... I have
> to tell you that when we do return, it will be without
> our beloved Lola. Lola has been stolen from us ... by
> a most distinguished citizen of Hamburg. I refer to
> none other than Professor – Immanuel – Raat!

Calls for Lola.

LOLA comes forward and sings '*Auf Wiedersehn*' – bidding farewell to HANS and LUTZ in the audience.

She steps back past the troupe, which is flanked by PAUL on one side and the PROFESSOR on the other.

LOLA joins the PROFESSOR's side for the last reprise.

He swells triumphant, his arm about her.

LOLA looks across at PAUL. He gazes at her, stone-faced.

Fade to black

END OF ACT ONE.

ACT TWO

ACT TWO - SCENE ONE.

The Plage at Nice.

The PROFESSOR, in resort clothes, is restless, waiting for LOLA. After a moment, she appears, with packages.

LOLA
Well, you silly old thing. What are you looking like that for?

PROFESSOR
I have been waiting for over an hour.

LOLA
Oh, is he hungry? *(She dives into one of the packages.)*

PROFESSOR
Not too many dresses I hope?

LOLA
For you!

She produces a boater, puts it on his head at a rakish angle. He tries to back off.

LOLA
No, wait! *(She takes out a bright cravat, and arranges it around his neck.)* There! Now you look the thing.

PROFESSOR
But ...

LOLA

You want to look young, don't you?

PROFESSOR

I will look as you wish me to look.

LOLA

Good.

PROFESSOR

But my dearest dear, please understand. My pocket is not without limit. These months together, never in my life did I dream of such ... of such ...

LOLA

Happiness?

PROFESSOR

Precisely the word I was seeking. Nonetheless, beloved enchantress, I must warn you that this morning, I received a letter from the bank. It seems that our funds are now low. Extremely low. We must, for example, move to a smaller hotel.

LOLA

If you say so.

PROFESSOR

I do say so.

LOLA

All right then. *(But there is a silence.)*

PROFESSOR

We cannot ... honeymoon forever. Your husband must provide for you. Find work.

ACT TWO

LOLA

But you've written to all the schools. They don't even answer. It's no good, sweetie, you're not respectable anymore.

PROFESSOR

I am a Doctor of Philosophy and Professor of Comparative Literature from the University of Heidelberg. My credentials and qualifications speak for me. I have decided to teach privately, and I shall set up my plate where my record of achievement is best known.

LOLA

You don't mean go back to Hamburg?

PROFESSOR

Why not? The prospect is invigorating. Let the town see what a fine woman I have married. It will take time, I concede, my dearest, to form a social circle. But we shall prevail. I give myself full marks.

LOLA

Just the same, why Hamburg? Why not stay here, in the warm?

PROFESSOR

And allow them to win? No! You are my wife. There will be no door closed against you. I give you my oath. Within a year, you will have the entrée to every drawing room, every salon, in the city. Even the Mayor himself.

LOLA

(*Flat*) Oh, good.

PROFESSOR
Trust me. And now we shall find a modest café in the town to eat our luncheon.

He comes close, to pick up her packages, and begins to murmur into her neck.

LOLA
Manny, not now. I'm hungry!

She kisses him on the nose. He can refuse her nothing.

LOLA
Something delicious, hmm? We can be sensible tomorrow.

Mesmerised, he follows her off along the plage.

Light change.

ACT TWO - SCENE TWO.

The Blue Angel.

BOMBLER is on his feet, trying to rouse his audience into joining him in a chorus of 'In Hamburg and Bremen and Lubeck.'

BERTHA and TUMTUM are in the wings.

He becomes frantic with failure, waves to the BAND who end abruptly, and in disorder, as he signals like a windmill.

BOMBLER
Pack it in! No good singing to thin air.

He stands, dismal and depressed.

TUMTUM
(*Little voice*) We need Lola, Uncle.

ACT TWO

BERTHA

They want Lola, guv.

He gives them a murderous look and goes.

Light change.

ACT TWO – SCENE THREE.

Hamburg.

FRAU PFLUG steps forward.

FRAU PFLUG

Of course, I couldn't honour the Professor's request to take up his rooms again. Not with ... How could I have such a woman under my roof? Still, I packed his things properly, his books, his laundry. *(With a little gleam of triumph)* Who would have thought it?!

Lights up on:

A Dull Room in A Rented Apartment.

The room has been made comfortable by Lola with cushions, and scarves over the lights, giving a sensuous atmosphere, offset by packing cases and the Professor's strapped PILES OF BOOKS.

PAUL and LOLA are in the centre of the room.

PAUL

Leave him!

She shrugs.

PAUL

He should clear out.

LOLA

I know. I tell him.

PAUL

Hans is leaving Hamburg next week for Berlin. Why don't you and I...

LOLA

Sssh, he's coming!

PAUL

Where can we meet?

She raises her hands at him.

The PROFESSOR enters and stops short at the sight of PAUL.

PROFESSOR

Eberhardt.

LOLA

Baron von Eberhardt has...

PROFESSOR

To what, may I ask, do we owe this honour?

PAUL

I came to pay my respects, to you and Frau Raat. *(He bows.)*

PROFESSOR

Very civil of you, to be sure.

LOLA

Aren't you going to offer the Baron something, Immanuel? He tells me he's at Heidelberg now.

PROFESSOR

You passed your examinations?

ACT TWO

PAUL

Cum laude. I should like to offer you this, with my gratitude.

He offers a small parcel. The PROFESSOR looks at him suspiciously, and takes out a book.

PAUL

Dostoevsky. A first edition. In translation, of course.

PROFESSOR

(His face darkens) Dostoevsky? That heathen jailbird? *(He throws the book aside.)* How dare you insult my hearth with such profanity?

PAUL

(Genuine) I'm sorry ...

PROFESSOR

I see through you. I have always seen through you. When others misbehaved, you did not. Why? You may answer.

PAUL says nothing.

PROFESSOR

You see? The same insolence.

PAUL

I'm sorry you feel that. *(He glances at the book on the floor.)*

PROFESSOR

Get out.

He stands by the door.

PAUL bows formally to LOLA. She picks up his book, and gives it back to him.

PAUL

(*At the door, to the PROFESSOR*) I have the honour, sir, to be, sir, your most obedient servant.

He bows frigidly and goes.

PROFESSOR

You see? More offence. How long was he here?

LOLA

Just arrived this minute. What's the matter?

PROFESSOR

Insults and humiliation. It is beyond bearing! I have given my life to this town. No man could have been more respected on the streets of Hamburg. Every hat was lifted. Now, my subscription from the Lodge demanded, and the tradesmen refuse credit. Why? Am I a defaulter? Have I been derelict in duty, in obligation? Have I, in any manner, acted with dishonour? No! I have done what is the privilege of any normal citizen. I have chosen to marry.

LOLA

You married me, Manny. (*She lights a cigarette.*)

PROFESSOR

Please do not call me that.

LOLA shrugs.

PROFESSOR

I have been kept waiting. I have been snubbed. I was even shown the door. Why?

LOLA

Because you're one of us now.

He looks up, frowning suspiciously.

ACT TWO

LOLA

One of the unacceptables. Too ugly, or too poor, or too timid to push for a seat on the tram. You've joined a popular club.

PROFESSOR

I will not tolerate this treatment. I shall have my revenge!

LOLA

(Shrewdly) Well, there's more than one way to kill a cat.

PROFESSOR

(Takes her hand) I will do anything. Anything to make them accept you.

LOLA

You bet. *(She thrusts a bill under his nose)* And if we don't pay this by tomorrow night, we shan't have a bed to sleep in. The landlord's sending his brothers to kick us out.

PROFESSOR

Insolence!

LOLA

You think they won't?

PROFESSOR

What is to be done?

LOLA

Leave it to me.

Light change.

ACT TWO – SCENE FOUR.

LOLA, in déshabille, sits in the light with an OLDER MAN.

The PROFESSOR hides behind a screen. The MAN becomes ardent. The PROFESSOR leaps out, pointing a gun with shaking hands.

LOLA screams.

At the same time, at The Blue Angel, DIETER assists KLAUS into a straitjacket, and fastens the buckles.

KLAUS, over a few minutes, struggles and writhes to escape.

>PROFESSOR
>Doktor Lippmann!

>LOLA
>It's my husband! Don't shoot ... oh please, don't shoot!

>>*Blackout.*

ACT TWO – SCENE FIVE.

The PROFESSOR and LOLA are alone. She is counting money and putting it into a large, black metal cash box. She finishes, shuts the box, and looks up, smiling.

>LOLA
>You see? Now we're safe. For the moment.

>PROFESSOR
>*(Mutters)* Never ask this of me again.

>LOLA
>Why not? You were very good.

ACT TWO

PROFESSOR

(Shudders) No. Not even for you. Everything. My life, my reputation – everything I am is invested here.

LOLA

Some investment. They've used you! Well, now it's your turn.

PROFESSOR

(Silencing her with a wave of his hand.) Non-sequitur. False argument. An eye for an eye? *(He shakes his head.)* You think I am not aware of chicanery? Of misuse of trust? Of bad behaviour? I know the men of this town. They were my students, all of them. Do you think I didn't smell out the criminals before their voices broke? The untrustworthy, those who must win, must crow on the manure heap? I tell you, I, Professor Raat, know the weaknesses of every man of substance in this town.

LOLA

O-oh? *(She looks up alertly interested.)* Do you, mein Herr? Do you?

PROFESSOR

Certainly. Nonetheless, I believe – I fully believe – that our beloved city can only be fuelled by civic virtue. It is true that there are times when we may be forced to employ those we despise to run our affairs. Those whose avaricious energy thrusts them up ...

LOLA

Including your ex-friends?

He frowns at her interruption.

LOLA

From the Lodge – the Law Society? *(She waves her little black book towards him.)* I know them too, remember?

He reacts.

LOLA

And for your good behaviour and honourable obedience, what reward, Professor? A piece of ribbon? A chiming clock?

PROFESSOR

No reward is necessary for a life of genuine service.

LOLA

Just so long as you realise you've been fooled. *(She closes on him.)* At least you know now, before it's too late. *(Softly)* Let them win? Time to play them at their own game, Manny.

He looks at her aghast, as her meaning sinks in.

PROFESSOR

(Whispers) I am to join the regiment of criminals? Debase myself? Knowingly ... consciously ... willingly? No! I refuse!

LOLA

(Quietly) You're not in a position to refuse.

PROFESSOR

My dear ...

LOLA

I don't intend to walk the streets for you, my friend.

PROFESSOR

But ...

ACT TWO

LOLA

If you think you can sit there counting the money while I ...

PROFESSOR

Stop! Please! My dearest one. How could you think ... that you could believe ... even dream of putting me into such a category?

LOLA

Why not? You're a man, aren't you?

Angry, she swipes over a pile of his books.

PROFESSOR

Please. Trust me. I will prove worthy as your husband. I will provide for you.

LOLA

How?

PROFESSOR

Very well. The politics of necessity. Force majeure. What is necessary for survival shall be done.

With a last, thrilling look, she leaves.

The PROFESSOR stands, immobile, for a long moment.

Light change

ACT TWO – SCENE SIX.

The Blue Angel.

The TROUPE march forward with their militaristic version of *'Happy Days are Here Again.'*

Meanwhile...

Lola's Bedroom.

LOLA is en déshabille with an OLD MAN. The PROFESSOR enters with a gun.

LOLA
It's my husband! Don't shoot! Don't shoot!

Instrumental '*Happy Days are Here Again.*'

As the cabaret continues, in the bedroom LOLA is with ANOTHER MAN. The PROFESSOR enters, as before.

LOLA
It's my husband! Don't shoot, don't shoot!

In the Blue Angel, the cabaret reaches a climax.

'*Happy Days are Here Again.*' reprise, full cabaret.

BOMBLER and the PROFESSOR enter, in conversation.

BOMBLER
Times are bad, Herr Professor. Now if Lola could come back to the Blue Angel...

PROFESSOR
I shall buy the Blue Angel for her. It is her wish.

BOMBLER goggles.

MAI sings and DIETER plays in accompaniment. '*Liebe Ohne Liebe.*'

BOMBLER
I've set up the gaming tables, sir.

PROFESSOR
Excellent.

BOMBLER
What we really need is Lola.

ACT TWO

KLAUS and HERMINE finally perform their Apache dance.

PROFESSOR

For two years now, Mr Mayor, you have defaulted on your gaming debts. Enough.

MAYOR

But you've cleaned me out. I have no funds.

PROFESSOR

Then you must expect the consequences.

BOMBLER

Could you reconsider, sir? Let Lola perform!

In the Blue Angel, MAI, BERTHA and TUMTUM attempt to provide the Lola ingredient, with BOMBLER's assistance. '*Kinde Heut Abend.*'

PROFESSOR

Come now, Herr Pressmann, surely the information in my hands will persuade you? Be good enough to transfer the bonds.

PRESSMANN

But that's blackmail!

PROFESSOR

(Thunders) Do as I say sir. Today!

The full cabaret re-emerges to sing the climax of their show.

The TWO FAT GIRLS run on with hoops. HERMINE does cartwheels. KLAUS and DIETER run on tumbling and juggling, topped by BOMBLER on a unicycle, blowing a horn.

'*Happy Days are Here Again*' (reprise), ending with HERMINE doing the splits and the GIRLS holding their hoops high.

As they leave, BOMBLER, with KLAUS, brings the JUDGE to the backstage area.

> JUDGE
>
> I must protest! This is hardly the place!

> BOMBLER
>
> Wait here.

The JUDGE looks around, agitated. The PROFESSOR appears and observes him from the shadows.

> PROFESSOR
>
> Good evening, Helmut.

The JUDGE jumps. The PROFESSOR comes forward.

> PROFESSOR
>
> You were trying, I believe, an interesting case today. A glass of wine ... no? It's a fine Bordeaux. A man accused of – what was it? – an attack on a defenceless woman?

> JUDGE
>
> (*Waves his hand, refusing a drink*) I have another engagement. I came to tell you that what you ask is impossible.

The PROFESSOR sits, and drinks without haste.

> PROFESSOR
>
> Indeed.

> JUDGE
>
> Herr Professor, be reasonable.

> PROFESSOR
>
> A simple request. My reinstatement as an honorary member of the Law Society.

ACT TWO

JUDGE

Utterly impossible.

PROFESSOR

I beg to differ. With your influence ...

JUDGE

My dear sir, no influence by me or anyone else could help you. Your altered state ...

PROFESSOR

What do you mean? I am legally married. There is no irregularity in my ...

JUDGE

Herr Raat!

PROFESSOR

Herr Doktor Raat!

JUDGE

I beg your pardon. But you will allow me to point out that apart from the question of your marriage, it is, to say the very least, unusual for a full Professor of Literature and Philosophy to be the owner of ... of a drinking establishment in the docklands area of Hamburg.

PROFESSOR

The club belongs to my wife.

JUDGE

Precisely.

Silence.

PROFESSOR

Very well. Since you choose to do nothing for me, I am forced to ask you for cash.

JUDGE

No, no. None of that, if you please.

The JUDGE moves to go. BOMBLER and KLAUS stand in his way.

The PROFESSOR takes a set of photographs out of his cash box. The JUDGE looks at them and falls into a chair with shock.

JUDGE

(Low) How were these taken?

The PROFESSOR smiles, enjoying his ascendancy.

JUDGE

Who has the negatives?

PROFESSOR

I do. Here. In my breast pocket.

JUDGE

Are these the only prints?

PROFESSOR

They are. You have my word.

The JUDGE looks at him sharply. But his eyes fall on the pictures again, and he collapses back in his chair, beaten.

Silence.

JUDGE

(Mutters) How much do you want?

The PROFESSOR hands him a slip of paper.

JUDGE

That is quite impossible. I have nowhere near such funds.

PROFESSOR

I think so. If you sell your house.

ACT TWO

JUDGE

Sell my house? But what reason can I give, how can I explain?

The PROFESSOR, in a rage, bangs the table.

PROFESSOR

Reinstatement! I demand reinstatement!

The JUDGE rises and backs away.

JUDGE

I can do nothing.

PROFESSOR

(Sullen) The money then. *(Bangs table)* I must have it! The generosity is mine. You can be saved. You, who are guilty! You can repurchase your good name. I, who am guiltless ...

JUDGE

Guiltless?

PROFESSOR

(Softly) Have I, Herr Judge, sought to plunder thirteen-year old virgins?

The JUDGE blanches, and exits quickly.

PROFESSOR

(Calls after him) One month, Your Honour ... one month!

He crosses, with his cash box. DIETER, in the shadows, watches.

BOMBLER

(Announcement) Meine Damen und Herren. After being away from us for far too long, tonight she returns. I give you, your own Blue Angel. Lola!!

LOLA appears and sings '*Mein Blondes Baby.*'

PAUL, at his table, never takes his eyes from her.

She crosses to her Dressing Room.

In the dressing room, PAUL helps LOLA into her kimono, then sits on the sofa. She crosses, and sits at her dressing table. He watches her, then looks about him.

> LOLA
>
> What is it?
>
> PAUL
>
> So strange. The Blue Angel ... you ... me ... Hamburg ... as before.
>
> LOLA
>
> I'd rather be in the south ... in the sun.

He watches her with her make-up.

> PAUL
>
> No-o. No, you belong here, amid the ice and the snow. (*He crosses, bends and kisses her bare shoulder.*) My cold, white star.

She turns on him abruptly, and kisses him almost savagely.

> LOLA
>
> There! Was that cold?
>
> PAUL
>
> Yes. Very cold.

Disconcerted, she turns away.

> PAUL
>
> Have you never been in love?

ACT TWO

LOLA

Of course. Hundreds of times.

PAUL

I think not.

LOLA

I was once. With my father.

PAUL

Is he dead?

LOLA

(Bleak) To me he is. *(She turns, with a smile.)* Don't worry about it.

PAUL

I could melt the ice in your heart.

LOLA

You? What makes you so different?

PAUL

You like me.

She frowns, turns away.

PAUL

Shall I make you love me?

LOLA

Certainly not.

PAUL

Oh. Why?

LOLA

As you say, I like you.

PAUL

Come away with me. Come to Vienna! We could leave tomorrow. Be there the next morning. Leave him!

LOLA

I can't.

PAUL

Why not?

LOLA

This place, for one thing. It's in my name.

PAUL

That's just a front. He'll never let you have it. Come to Vienna. Please. Say yes.

LOLA

Even if the Danube is a dirty grey?

They embrace.

LOLA

Oh, damn you.

PAUL

You'll come with me – yes?

LOLA

Quick, it's him!

PAUL

But are you coming?

LOLA

Go!

PAUL

Not until you say yes.

ACT TWO

LOLA

What time's the train?

PAUL

Ten o'clock.

The PROFESSOR comes in, carrying a package. He's been drinking. He stops at the sight of PAUL.

PROFESSOR

You! What are you doing here?

PAUL

I'm asking your wife to run away with me.

A dreadful silence.

PROFESSOR

What? What?! *(It seems that he will strike PAUL but he stops suddenly.)* At last. You see? I was right. The insolence was always there. Now it comes out.

He laughs, waving the package in PAUL's face.

PAUL turns to go.

PROFESSOR

No, stay, Excellency. *(To LOLA)* A small token of my regard. Open it.

LOLA opens the box, lifts out a green necklace high.

PAUL gasps with surprise.

PAUL

But ... those are my mother's emeralds!

PROFESSOR

Correct. *(He fastens the necklace round her neck.)* And we are now in a position to purchase.

PAUL gapes at the necklace.

> LOLA
>
> Purchase? *(She frowns at PAUL, puzzled.)* Purchase what?

> PROFESSOR
>
> Why ... *(He cannot stop laughing)* ... why ... the Eberhardt house! His house!

> PAUL
>
> My house?

> PROFESSOR
>
> In payment.

> PAUL
>
> Payment? For what?

> PROFESSOR
>
> For every incivility shown to me by you, by your father, by your verdammt family. Oh, so civil always! So kind! So unfailingly courteous! *(He sweeps a drunken bow.)*

> PAUL
>
> Have you gone mad?

> LOLA
>
> What's he done, Count von Eberhardt?

> PROFESSOR
>
> *(Laughs)* Done? He hasn't done anything! *(He laughs, enjoying their bewilderment. Stops laughing)* But his brother has. Don't go, Excellency!

> LOLA
>
> What's the feller been up to?

ACT TWO

PROFESSOR

Fraud. They're all frauds, these Pillars of Society! *(He brandishes a large book.)* A new register. *(He turns the pages)* Cheats ... embezzlers ... fornicators ... *(He licks a finger, turns page.)* ... murderers. In alphabetical order.

Silence.

PAUL

And you make your living out of them?

PROFESSOR

By my own enterprise! You were right, liebling. For thirty years I was a fool. Others became rich. My reward was the success of my pupils. I was respected. I ate at the Mayor's table. Professor Immanuel Raat. Decorations will be worn. And what did it mean, this respect? It meant *nothing! (He looks at them both malevolently.)* This ... *(He slaps his hand on the cash box)* This is what matters! Money. Money creates ... Money controls! With money, I insist! I, Raat, insist! With money, I shall repurchase that which has been stolen from me.

PAUL

What?

PROFESSOR

Respect! Honour!

PAUL

By ruining my family?

PROFESSOR

I want my place! Frau Raat, my spouse, will preside over the finest staircase in Hamburg. *(To PAUL)*

You have been there long enough! Time to vacate!
(*Gestures*) My liebling will wear the finest furs,
jewels such as this city has never seen ... pearls,
ropes of pearls ... rubies, burning on your throat
like lava ... (*Turns to PAUL*) ... and I shall sit on
the terrace of the finest house in Hamburg – the
Eberhardt house – and watch her become the Queen of
the North.

PAUL

(*Pause*) They won't allow you to succeed in this.

He bows to LOLA, and goes.

PROFESSOR

(*Calls*) But I have succeeded! (*He closes on LOLA
amorously.*) My beloved – (*kisses her neck*) ... this is
what I bring you. Oh, dreams! I have such dreams!
Every night, a salon. The finest minds in Germany at
our table. And after, I am left with my prize. I shall
carry you up that celestial staircase ...

He suddenly clutches his chest, in pain. Grunts.

LOLA

You old silly! You've overdone it. Go on. I don't want
you tired for my party.

He makes to pick up the box.

LOLA

Don't worry, I'll put those away. You gave me the
combination, remember?

PROFESSOR

(*Vague*) As you wish. Wear the emeralds tomorrow.
They'll all be here ... the clients!

ACT TWO

LOLA

Is that wise?

PROFESSOR

Just watch them, my darling. Watch them dance for your birthday. To my tune!

He laughs and goes.

DIETER emerges.

He and LOLA look at each other for a long moment.

She looks at the cash box, then back at DIETER. DIETER looks at the cash box, then at LOLA, to be sure of her meaning.

She nods slightly, and goes.

DIETER crosses, and picks up the cash box.

Blackout.

ACT TWO - SCENE SEVEN.

A Street in The Docklands Area.

HERR PRESSMAN enters and waits nervously.

The MAYOR approaches furtively, and joins him. After a beat, they are joined by the JUDGE. They huddle, whispering and tense.

DIETER appears from the shadows. They regard him anxiously. The JUDGE moves towards him. DIETER gives him a paper.

The JUDGE joins his friends.

JUDGE

(Reads under street lamp) 'Let me do this. If not, I shall kill him. If I kill him, it will all come out. Give me the money and I will bring the papers.'

PRESSMAN

Does he mean tonight?

MAYOR

(To DIETER) Tonight?

DIETER nods.

JUDGE

Yes, tonight. Bring everything. Accounts, records... photographs... As we arranged.

DIETER goes.

MAYOR

Can we trust him?

JUDGE

It's a small price to pay.

PRESSMANN

We must risk it.

MAYOR

Till tonight, then.

Blackout

ACT TWO

ACT TWO – SCENE EIGHT.

The Dressing Area at The Blue Angel.

BERTHA and TUMTUM are prinking as they dress for the night's performance.

KLAUS and BOMBLER move about, preparing their props.

> BOMBLER
>
> Where's Dieter?
>
> KLAUS
>
> Haven't seen him all day.
>
> BOMBLER
>
> Funny.

He and KLAUS sort out the ropes.

HERMINE, now a dreadful Flapper, practices the Charleston in a corner. BERTHA nudges TUMTUM as HERMINE gets it wrong.

MAI enters.

She crosses to BOMBLER and punches him in the face.

Caught off balance, he falls. He gets up and rubs his painful jaw without a murmur, and carries on tying his tie.

MAI starts to dress for the evening, her face thunderous.

> TUMTUM
>
> *(In a little voice.)* Sorry, Auntie.

MAI turns and swipes her.

TUMTUM goes down, then gets up and finishes dressing, her snivelling intensified by HERMINE's satisfied smile. She sniffs, getting on KLAUS's nerves.

KLAUS

Beer, anyone?

HERMINE

Yes, please!

HERMINE gets a shove from MAI, her mother.

BERTHA gives KLAUS some money from her purse.

KLAUS

The usual? *(BERTHA nods.)* Herr Bombler?

BOMBLER

Shut up. Now listen all of you. We've got the whole of Hamburg out there tonight! I want you all on your toes. I want you crisp. I want bounce. Above all, I want you debonair.

The PROFESSOR enters.

BOMBLER

Professor, sir! Everything in order?

PROFESSOR

I told you, tonight must be well-arranged.

MAI

He'll be here. We're trying our best, sir.

BOMBLER

We won't let you down ...

BERTHA

We've worked really hard ...

TUMTUM

For Lola's birthday. *(She withers in the PROFESSOR's glare.)*

ACT TWO

HERMINE

You mean, Frau Raat.

BERTHA

Frau Raat, she means.

PROFESSOR

Kindly remember to address your employer correctly. Otherwise you will be dismissed.

BERTHA

Oh, don't say that, sir!

TUMTUM

You wouldn't do that, sir!

He looks at them with disfavour and walks off, ignoring a curtsey from HERMINE.

MAI

I'll have his tripes for corset laces.

TUMTUM

Sssh, he'll hear you, Auntie!

BOMBLER

Come on, all of you – get to work.

MAI starts to play. BERTHA and TUMTUM line up lethargically and start a limp routine.

HERMINE attempts to flirt with KLAUS, who is drinking beer. She hangs round him as he drinks phlegmatically.

BOMBLER

(To the GIRLS) No, no, no! Not like that! *(He mutters furiously to himself.)* Come here. Not like that ... like this!

He bursts into a frenetic tap dance. The GIRLS watch, their eyes and mouths wide. MAI bangs out the last phrases, enlivened by BOMBLER'S energy.

The dance ends and BOMBLER heaves, out of breath.

An awed silence.

> TUMTUM
>
> That was good, Uncle.

Further silence as the GIRLS digest the implications.

> BERTHA
>
> You want us to do it like that, Mr Bombler?

> BOMBLER
>
> (*Breathless, he can hardly speak*) Yes ... like that ...

> BERTHA
>
> All right, then.

BERTHA exits.

> TUMTUM
>
> But ...

TUMTUM follows BERTHA off, perplexed.

> MAI
>
> Didn't know you had it in you.

> BOMBLER
>
> There's a lot you don't know, old girl. I'll prove it now if you like.

> MAI
>
> Ah. Well ... Only I've got to see to the band parts.

> BOMBLER
>
> Of course.

ACT TWO

MAI

Otherwise I'd ...

BOMBLER

Absolutely.

MAI

Here. Is this a good idea?

BOMBLER

What?

MAI

Inviting all the nobs. You don't think he's asking for trouble?

BOMBLER

No! He's putting us on the map.

MAI

There's some funny things being said.

BOMBLER

Things? What things?

MAI

About him. About what he gets up to.

BOMBLER

I should keep your mouth shut if I were you.

MAI

And what's all this stuff about expansion?

BOMBLER

Mind your own business. Where the hell is Dieter?

MAI

You want to watch out.

BOMBLER

What do you mean?

She jerks her head, meaning the Professor.

BOMBLER

He's an educated man. What's more, he's out to win!

MAI

And naturally you're included. Let me tell you something. When it's winners and losers, people are out for themselves. And for every winner there's a thousand losers. Stands to reason. Expansion! *(She laughs.)* I should be careful, mein Herr.

BOMBLER

Don't talk rubbish. We're doing well enough, aren't we?

MAI

Until we get caught.

BOMBLER

Caught? What do you mean, caught?

MAI

I hope you've got your suitcase packed. I have.

BOMBLER

Look at her! We've never been so well off, and she stands there grumbling. Look at this place ... new floor, new paint ... you wouldn't know it!

MAI

(Takes her sheet music and goes) The drains still smell though, don't they?

Blackout.

ACT TWO

ACT TWO – SCENE NINE.

The Blue Angel.

The JUDGE, the MAYOR and PRESSMANN enter. They leave their things with the HAT-CHECK GIRL and take their seats.

LOLA enters and sings 'Johnny.'

BOMBLER enters, and lifts his hands for silence.

BOMBLER
Ladies and gentlemen ... Gentlemen. Tonight ...
tonight, as you know, is a very special occasion.
We are celebrating the birthday of our one and
only ... of the star of The Blue Angel ... our beloved
enchantress ... Lola!

BERTHA and TUMTUM give LOLA a birthday cake and flowers.

BOMBLER
As you know, Lola ... Frau Raat ... is now our revered
employer. Lola ... with our love and thanks!

Applause.

LOLA
Thank you so much. I have a feeling tonight will be a
night to remember.

She crosses to meet the PROFESSOR. He kisses her hand, and they dance a waltz together. He stops, holds up his hand for silence.

PROFESSOR
Ladies and gentlemen. I am pleased to see so many of
our leading citizens, here tonight to honour my wife.
Any absentees, you may be sure, have been noted.
Among those present are ...

PRESSMANN

(Unseen) Herr Raat ...

MAYOR

(Unseen) Professor Raat ...

JUDGE

Officer, if you will.

A POLICEMAN steps forward.

POLICEMAN

Silence, if you please. On the orders of the police, this club is now closed. All of those present proceed to the nearest exit.

PROFESSOR

What? What are you doing? Stop it ... *(As people start to leave.)* Come back! Stop it, I say! Pay no attention to ...

POLICEMAN

Be quiet, please. *(Calls to those leaving.)* My men are outside. Be good enough to leave quietly and without incident.

PROFESSOR

What is this outrage? Why are you here? Do you know who I am?

POLICEMAN

Sir, we know who you are. And we know what you do.

PROFESSOR

What do you mean? By whose authority are you here? I demand that you leave these premises and allow my guests to return. This is an outrage!

ACT TWO

POLICEMAN

You are – *(consults his notebook)* – one Immanuel Gustav Raat?

PROFESSOR

I am Professor Doktor Raat and I insist that you give me a full explanation of your conduct.

POLICEMAN

(Quietly) I don't think you understand. I am placing you under arrest. Sir.

PROFESSOR

Arrest? Arrest? *(Bewildered, he turns to LOLA.)* On what charge?

The JUDGE, the MAYOR and HERR PRESSMANN step forward.

POLICEMAN

Illegal gambling.

PROFESSOR

Impossible. Impossible.

JUDGE

Herr Raat ...

MAYOR

Professor Raat ...

PRESSMANN

Herr Professor ...

They smile at him.

PROFESSOR

I see. I see. Well, well. So, it is to be defiance. Very unwise, gentlemen. Come, the joke has gone far enough.

MAYOR

A matter of possession, is it?

JUDGE

Possession, my dear Raat, is nine points of the law.

PROFESSOR

(As doubts begin, he mutters) Surely it is not in your interests to try me so far?

PAUL enters.

The MAYOR, PRESSMANN and the JUDGE bow to him.

PAUL

My apologies. I seem to have missed your celebrations. There was a matter for my father ... *(His voice breaks slightly)* ... for us to attend to. *(To the PROFESSOR)* Perhaps it will interest you. My uncle, Conrad von Eberhardt, was pulled from the river tonight.

A murmur of shock from his listeners.

PROFESSOR

And what is that to me? I feel no shame. The man was a fraud. If he prefers death to dishonour, why then ... then ...

DIETER enters, brandishing the cash box.

The JUDGE and PRESSMANN hold up the PROFESSOR's books.

PROFESSOR

My books! No! no, no, no, no, no!

The POLICEMAN hauls him away.

ACT TWO

PROFESSOR

No, I say, no! I am a German citizen ... you have no right! I am a Professor of the University of Heidelberg! You cannot arrest me! My wife. Where is my wife?!

He struggles violently but is manhandled offstage.

LOLA follows.

JUDGE

This establishment will be closed until further order.

The TROUPE are left alone.

KLAUS hands round cigarettes. MAI gets the packed suitcase.

BERTHA

Where's Lola?

TUMTUM

What's happened to Lola?

LOLA enters.

MAI

Didn't you go with him?

LOLA

What for?

MAI

I'd shove off if I were you.

There is a movement in the shadows. LOLA turns.

DIETER steps into the light.

LOLA

Hullo, Dieter. Good night?

He looks at her with a fleeting smile.

                    LOLA

Where's the cashbox?

He produces the cash box, opens it slowly, and throws handfuls of notes into the air. LOLA stands back, laughing, as the OTHERS scramble for the money.

                    LOLA

Hey, leave some for me!

The TROUPE scurry away with the money.

                  HERMINE

Mutti, are we stopping or going?

                    MAI

We'll see, we'll see!

DIETER offers the open cash box to LOLA but she shakes her head.

She reaches up, kisses him gently on the cheek. He gives her a long look, then glances across to PAUL, standing apart. DIETER bows briefly to LOLA, with one last look, and goes, with the box under his arm.

LOLA looks after him.

                    LOLA

'Bye, Dieter.

DIETER's step falters, then he continues on his way.

LOLA turns, taking off the emerald necklace.

She holds it out to PAUL.

He ignores it, takes her by the hand and leads her to the bedroom.

Light change.

ACT TWO

ACT TWO - SCENE TEN.

The Blue Angel. The next morning.

PAUL

(Calling up to the bedroom) Breakfast is served, my lady.

LOLA

(From upstairs) Oh, come back ...

PAUL

I can't, I'm late already. *(Calls)* What will you do?

LOLA

I don't know. And you?

PAUL

I shall stay for my Uncle's funeral.

LOLA comes downstairs in a dressing gown.

PAUL

There's nothing to keep you here. Let me take you, if not Vienna, then Rome – Madrid – the moon! We could be warm together. Coffee? Cake? Say yes!

LOLA

For how long?

PAUL

(Shrugs) Oh, until the autumn. I shall have to be back in Heidelberg for the Michaelmas term.

She takes out a cigarette. He lights it for her.

LOLA

I hear you became engaged. Nice girl?

PAUL

(*Dismissive*) It's not important.

LOLA

I daresay my husband's made it all the more necessary for you to marry the Essen steel industry.

PAUL

It needn't affect us.

She laughs drily.

PAUL

Please. Come away.

He shakes her hand gently to and fro.

LOLA

Why should I?

PAUL

Because it's finished here. And because you like me. (*He leans across the table, and kisses her.*) There, you see? Five icicles dropped from your nose. Say yes. Come with me.

LOLA

Until Michaelmas?

But she smiles at him briefly.

PAUL

You see? The ice is melting.

She rises, walks past him, and touches his hair briefly.

LOLA

Who would have thought it!

PAUL

(*Calls*) You will? (*He turns.*)

ACT TWO

She is looking at him sadly.

> **PAUL**
>
> What?
>
> **LOLA**
>
> Nothing.
>
> **PAUL**
>
> What is it?
>
> **LOLA**
>
> If you knew! *(She approaches him.)*
>
> **PAUL**
>
> Knew? Knew what? Tell me.
>
> **LOLA**
>
> Let's hope you're one of the lucky ones. Let's hope you never know.
>
> **PAUL**
>
> *(Puzzled)* Know what?
>
> **LOLA**
>
> Oh ... life.

She laughs. He doesn't.

> **PAUL**
>
> So, you won't come away with me? Is it because of him? Your husband? Because he's locked up?
>
> **LOLA**
>
> I need to know where I stand.

He stands over her, frowning. An idea occurs to him. He puts on his gloves with decision, and takes his cloak.

> **LOLA**
>
> Where are you going?

PAUL

(*Mutters*) There is something I can do.

LOLA

What?

But he has gone.

Blackout.

ACT TWO – SCENE ELEVEN.

KLAUS enters.

KLAUS

Lola? Lola? (*He sees LOLA sitting on the stairs.*) Oh. Evening, Lola.

LOLA

Play something.

KLAUS plays 'Auf Wiedersehn.' LOLA approaches and sings.

KLAUS breaks into 'Beware Blonde Women.' LOLA laughs wryly, pours herself a drink, waves the bottle at him, he shakes his head.

KLAUS

We might as well clear off. This place is finished.

LOLA

(*Thoughtful*) I wonder. It is in my name.

KLAUS

They'll still take it.

LOLA

They might not. The Mayor's an old acquaintance. And the Chief of Police.

ACT TWO

KLAUS

You'll be all right then.

LOLA

Under new management! Lola's!

Heads close, they both shine at the thought.

And both jump as the PROFESSOR enters, dishevelled and exhausted.

KLAUS

It's him!

LOLA

You're out! *(She waves KLAUS off.)*

KLAUS exits.

The PROFESSOR looks at her without answering. He seems collapsed.

LOLA

How did you manage it?

The PROFESSOR slumps onto a chair.

PROFESSOR

(Mutters) Eberhardt.

LOLA

What?

PROFESSOR

(Looks up malevolently) The Count von Eberhardt ... intervened.

Silence.

LOLA

After what you did to his brother?

> PROFESSOR
>
> There will be no court case.

Silence.

LOLA suddenly puts her hand to her mouth in realisation.

> LOLA
>
> So that was it!
>
> PROFESSOR
>
> *(Flash of rage)* The Count von Eberhardt behaves well because the Count von Eberhardt can afford to behave well!

PAUL enters.

> LOLA
>
> It wasn't him.
>
> PROFESSOR
>
> What?
>
> LOLA
>
> It wasn't the Count. It was his son – Paul. Paul, your favourite pupil. *(Quietly)* Here is your Siegfried.

The PROFESSOR's expression alters. He glares at her and comes forward in a rage. But he staggers and LOLA helps him to a chair.

PAUL approaches with a glass of water.

The PROFESSOR waves him away angrily.

> LOLA
>
> *(Low)* Leave him to me.

PAUL moves apart.

ACT TWO

PROFESSOR

(Grasps LOLA's hand, and stares up at her fervently)
Swear! Swear that you will be loyal.

LOLA

(Puzzled) Loyal?

PROFESSOR

I will provide for you. Trust me.

LOLA moves away.

LOLA

We lost.

PROFESSOR

Another town. A new beginning.

LOLA

No. It's over.

PROFESSOR

Over?

LOLA

Yes.

PROFESSOR

Never. You are my wife, I demand your allegiance.
You bear my name.

LOLA

My name is Lola.

PROFESSOR

You have no loyalty? Your love then ...

LOLA

Love? I've no love.

PROFESSOR

But you love me! You have said so.

LOLA

I'm a liar. You married beneath you, Professor. You should have stuck to your school. Not that they didn't hate you there. Still, they could come to me for comfort.

PROFESSOR

No love?

LOLA

It's not something I know about.

PROFESSOR

You have no feeling for me?

LOLA

I have some feeling.

PROFESSOR

But if you feel, is that not love?

LOLA

I pity you.

Silence. He seems to swell. He advances on her.

PROFESSOR

You? Pity me? How dare you! How dare you? I forbid it. A woman such as you – you dare to pity me, Professor Immanuel Raat, of the University of Heidelberg? I think you have forgotten your place.

LOLA looks up at him bleakly.

LOLA

This *is* my place.

ACT TWO

PROFESSOR

I will not be pitied. Whore, you have destroyed me!

He lifts a hand high, to strike her. And suddenly rears, almost to tiptoe. His face widens in a terrible grimace of pain.

He falls across her with a dreadful, expiring groan. She bends over him as, on his knees, he clutches at her.

PROFESSOR

Please ... please ... please ...

She looks down at him.

PROFESSOR

Please ...

He tries to speak, but can only make sounds. She puts her arms around him, and speaks in a thrilling, soft voice.

LOLA

Of course, I love you ... I'll always love you ... no-one else, just you, only you. Mein Mann. We'll go away to the sun as we did before. We'll go south, where it's warm. We'll be together. We'll be happy. That's what you want, isn't it? You want to be happy, that's what you want.

Her voice dies away. She sees that he is dead.

She flinches momentarily away from him, then lets him down gently, holding his head.

LOLA

It's what we all want. To be happy.

She and PAUL stand by the body. PAUL puts out a hand. LOLA does not take it.

LOLA

Go home, Paul.

PAUL

Why? You're free. We can have what we want.

LOLA

What *you* want?

PAUL

What we both want.

LOLA looks down briefly at the PROFESSOR, and moves away.

PAUL

Lola? I don't believe your heart is cold.

LOLA

Then you're a fool.

PAUL

What *do* you want?

LOLA

To survive. Survive him. You. Go home, Paul.

They regard each other for a long, hopeless moment.

Then he turns and goes.

LOLA crosses. She sings: '*Falling in Love Again.*' ('Ich Bin von Kopf Bis Fuss Auf Liebe Eingestellt')

The End.

LOVING WOMEN

For Phil Davis

LOVING WOMEN was first performed on the 31st of January, 1984, at the Arts Theatre, Great Newport Street, London, UK. Produced by JONATHAN GEMS and DAVID JONES, directed by PHILIP DAVIS, designed by JONATHAN GEMS.

CAST

Susannah	MARION BAILEY
Frank	DAVID BEAMES
Crystal	GWYNETH STRONG
Production Manager	TONY HARPUR
Stage Manager	EVELYN DOGGART
Costume Designer	KATE BURNETT
Lighting Designer	STEPHEN ROLFE
Costume Designer	MAGGIE BINOUX
Production Assistant	CHRISTINE HARMAR-BROWN
Production Coordinator	SARAH WEBSTER
Photography	MARK RUSHER
Publicity	JIMEX

REVIEWS

In the second act of what strikes me as being Pam Gems's best play to date, Green Peace-teaching wimp, Frank, is discomfited behind the apricot sofa, and deposited, clutching his groin, in a pose by the Windscale and Crisis In Capitalism wall charts. His loving women – working class hairdresser Crystal and Birmingham communard (recently returned from Bolivia) Susannah – forge a new alliance on the aforementioned sofa.

The interval brought us to this pretty pass, i.e. the present, after scenes of territorial manoeuvering (yes, they do mention Robert Ardrey) in the early 70s ... The Mao poster gives way to Marc Bolan. Lou Reed paves the way on the soundtrack; the bead doorway and Indian carpet cede to the arrival of a drinks trolley (two kinds of sherry) and the baby.

The baby is Crystal's and Frank's. Susannah, who lived with Frank for five years, now turns on him for having joined the Labour Party. He is also, good grief, wearing a wine velvet jacket. Driven like a wedge through these flickering displays of middle-class guilt, reaction and muddled purpose, is the undeniably coarse working class heroine – uncomplicated by trauma or paperback philosophy – the hairdresser. In this role, Gwyneth Strong is absolutely superb ...

There are some excellent speeches. Frank's tribute to Crystal's body and reproductive instincts is beautifully delivered by David Beames ... Marion Bailey is tremendous as Susannah, judging perfectly the thin line between satiric intention and sympathetic pitch ...

Pam Gems has invested this contemporary comedy of manners with some stirring emotional insights. The materialistic marital squabbles are eerily convincing. The portrait of a disenchanted middle-class career leftie yearning for a child is one of the most poignant images of our recent theatre.

> MICHAEL COVENEY *Financial Times*. 02/02/1984

It is a long time since I saw a new comedy which delighted me as much. Pam Gems's LOVING WOMEN at the ARTS is just the winter tonic we have been waiting for: sexually knowing, wittily in touch with young people's lifestyles and, above all, funny.

This is something more than a contemporary love-triangle, with two girls after the same chap. It catches the old, defiant, freedom-asserting mood of the 1970s, and then leaps to the present to show a social recalcitrance being born in an England torn between Puritanism and class nastiness.

We begin with serious, attractive Frank in bed, being fussed over by serious, attractive Susannah. He has been ill, but her work had compelled her to leave his nursing to capable Crystal – a dizzy, working-class blonde armed with vitality, a delicious body, and home-cooking.

For five year, Frank and Susannah, both educationalists, have toiled for the Communist dream. She cannot believe it when he suddenly departs, marries her rival, and reneges on their shared principles for the sake of a baby, a home, and an uneducated sex-pot.

In a great quarrel scene, he explains that the materialist, ugly, dead-end campaigning had died on him. Contemptuously, she accuses him of detaching himself from the human race and takes herself abroad to do good works among the needy and deprived.

We rush back eagerly after the interval – and how often does that happen? – to catch the trio ten years later, to find Susannah, just back home, begging Frank to give her a child. She would like him too, and is not displeased to learn that Crystal is restless, unfaithful, and bored.

The play climaxes in a tremendous fight, but the outcome is totally unexpected. Rising triumphantly, above the bruises and black eyes, soars the indomitable Crystal, to sweep them all towards a solution likely to reconcile Susannah's procreative needs with Frank's bourgeois instincts and her own larkish promiscuity.

In this role, Gwyneth Strong gives an endearing performance, flaunting like a butterfly in one provocative outfit after another, but rock steady inside. David Beames catches Frank's good sense as well as his humourlessness, while Marion Bailey suggests an idealist who is not also a prig.

Like all good comedies, this is a little more. It understands the raw pain in the agonized choices and yearnings that obsess the young. But, without compromising any of their urgency, it weaves them into a sexual situation which amuses and surprises throughout.

JOHN BARBER. The *Daily Telegraph*. 02/02/1984

No one can accuse Pam Gems of short-changing her audience in her new play LOVING WOMEN at the ARTS THEATRE.

In the space of a couple of hours, she gaily touches upon virtually every subject which has found favour with committed dramatists in recent years.

The failure of revolutionary politics, the plight of the Third World, the women's movement, the short-comings of The

Pill, ecology, Greenham Common, and the new orthodoxy of the Right – if it's a fashionable theme, you can confidently bet that Pam Gems has got it in there.

This, in short, is a voluble muddle of a play but it remains a stubbornly enjoyable one. Though, at times, one experiences the desperate feeling of being cornered by a group of opinionated bores at a party, the dramatist provides the saving grace of humour.

She views her characters with a mixture of compassion and malevolence, exposing their absurdities even as one sympathises with their plight. The arguments may be half-baked but the people are only too recognisably real.

LOVING WOMEN explores that familiar terrain, the romantic triangle. The action opens in a London flat in the early seventies where the left wing social worker, Frank, is laid-up with a nervous collapse. With his equally revolutionary, and equally middle-class, mistress away patronising the working classes in Birmingham, he quickly succumbs to the curvaceous charms of the cockney hairdresser, Crystal.

With a child on the way, Frank marries his crimper and the play then jumps forward ten years to the present day, when the relationships are resolved in a violent and surprisingly funny confrontation.

The director, Philip Davis, makes the most of the often black humour and is greatly helped by a richly comic performance from Gwyneth Strong as the highly-sexed, cynical hairdresser.

Marion Bailey plays the suffering socialist, Susannah, with exactly the right kind of irritating earnestness, while David Beames succeeds in making the audience care about Frank, even as they laugh at him.

CHARLES SPENCER. The *Evening Standard*. 02/02/1984

LOVING WOMEN

ACT ONE

ACT ONE – SCENE ONE.

The interior of a flat, 1973. The bed is on the floor, a mattress with an old eiderdown over. Furniture is sparse, but there is a hi-fi with large twin speakers. Political or ethnic posters, including Ché and Mao.

A man sits up in bed, propped up with cushions. There is something worrying about him ... something sharp, intense, melancholy, even dangerous. He looks ill. His face is pale under the beard. This is FRANK.

The young woman sitting on the floor and leaning over him is thin and angular in tight, faded jeans. She is not particularly good-looking or noticeable until her face becomes alive with humour or feeling. She wears a battered old anorak, has an enormous cloth shoulder-bag weighed down with books and papers. This is SUSANNAH.

She leans over FRANK, groping in her bag with a smile, then presents him with a record, looking at his face to register his pleasure.

He takes it and looks at it neutrally.

> FRANK

Oh ... thanks.

> SUSANNAH

I knew you'd want it.

FRANK

Yuh.

SUSANNAH

Quite a job to get it – sold out!

He nods, inspecting the sleeve.

SUSANNAH

Well. So. How's it going?

CRYSTAL enters.

CRYSTAL

Hey you're not gonna talk about work, are you?

She is dazzling, young and fresh with long limbs and shining hair, her clothes bang on fashion.

SUSANNAH

No, no.

CRYSTAL

Only 'e's not s'posed to.

SUSANNAH

Sure.

CRYSTAL

The doctor said no worry.

SUSANNAH

Sure. Great. No ... everything's okay. The department's coping all right. Well enough for you not to worry. Not so well that you aren't missed, of course. (*She puts her hand on her heart.*) 'It ain't the same, mate!'

FRANK

What are you doing?

ACT ONE

SUSANNAH

Oh, a fantastic new scheme. We're involving *all* the kids – music, design, dance. Everybody involved. We're after total interdependence. (*Hugs him.*) Natural follow-on from you, love.

FRANK

Sounds quite a big thing.

CRYSTAL

Come *on*! 'E's not supposed to talk about it!

SUSANNAH

Oh ... sorry! No, great ... Sorry, Crystal! How's she been as a nurse?

FRANK

Fine. Beautiful pair of knockers bending over me, I have to feel good.

He reaches for a cigarette, and CRYSTAL quickly gets up and lights it for him. SUSANNAH notices that he is smoking, and shakes her head, frowning slightly.

FRANK draws gratefully on the cigarette and picks up the disc, examining the sleeve.

SUSANNAH

Do you want to hear it?

FRANK

Yeah.

She hands him the headphones, crosses, and puts on the record. FRANK, wearing the headphones, nods and smiles briefly.

SUSANNAH and CRYSTAL move apart for a chat.

SUSANNAH

How is he?

CRYSTAL

Not too grand.

SUSANNAH

He looks terrible. Thanks a bundle, Crystal. It's really great of you. I'd no idea it was going to be such a chore.

CRYSTAL

Don't worry about it.

SUSANNAH

I feel awful.

CRYSTAL

No, I enjoy it, honest. Gives me somefing to do at nights. Least I don't go out spendin' money. Anyway, for God's sake, you done me a favour! Couldn't wait to get out of that squat.

SUSANNAH

Squitty?

CRYSTAL

I had to clean the whole place out so's me Mum could come and visit. Hey, she said, our Crystal ... you're never living in 'ere with all them fellers! Gave her the thrill of 'er life.

They laugh.

CRYSTAL

She needn't 'ave worried.

SUSANNAH

What do you mean?

ACT ONE

CRYSTAL

We-ell ...

SUSANNAH continues to look puzzled.

CRYSTAL

... they're all your sort, ain't they?

SUSANNAH

What do you mean?

CRYSTAL

They're all ... liberated. Puts you off, dunnit?

SUSANNAH

Oh. Why?

CRYSTAL

You know Harry? The one with the beard?

SUSANNAH

Tall?

CRYSTAL

No, that's Pete. His is all scratchy. No, the silky one ...

SUSANNAH lifts her head in a nod.

CRYSTAL

You don't know what you're getting. Mate of mine didn't half get a shock when her old man shaved off. He had a hare lip! They were married an' all! Anyway, this Harry asks me out for a burger. Nips in for a six-pack on the way 'ome. I fink 'Iyiy!' Back to the squat, he sits me down on one of them big cushions you keep rolling off of – starts pullin' off his boots and I think ... we-ell, 'e smells all right. You know, clean. Anyway, I get a bit of a cuddle. I'm just relaxing – fishing round for it – when, all of a sudden, he puts his mush in me ear and whispers: 'What would you like me to do, Crystal?'

They both burst out laughing.

SUSANNAH
(*Laughing*) What did you say?

CRYSTAL
I thought of a thing or two, I can tell you. 'Look,' 'e says. 'I'm not one of those geezers that jumps a gal. I'm not the bam-bam thank you ma'am type.' I said: 'Wot?' Got out the bloody cigarettes.

SUSANNAH
It put you off?

There is an objective curiosity in SUSANNAH's glance.

CRYSTAL
I thought 'e was gonna bring out the manual! Christ, what are they after? Good marks or somefing?

SUSANNAH
You like the man to take the lead?

CRYSTAL
Sure. Within reason. Tell you one thing, though, your lot's never gonna be up for rape.

SUSANNAH gives her another mild look – as at a specimen.

SUSANNAH
How long had you been there? At the squat?

CRYSTAL
I was only fillin' in till I got somewhere. I couldn't find nothing. It's ridiculous. I really love the room here.

ACT ONE

I'm ever so grateful. I mean, what with it bein' near the salon ...

SUSANNAH

Sure. Well, it's okay for now. I mean, when I get back, we'll have to ...

FRANK stirs, listening to the music.

CRYSTAL

Sssh. Did you say something, Frank?

FRANK lifts the headphones enquiringly.

CRYSTAL

Need anyfing?

He smiles, shakes his head, and puts back the headphones.

CRYSTAL

(*Lowering her voice.*) He's been ever so rough.

SUSANNAH

Oh? Why didn't you let me know?

CRYSTAL

He didn't want to.

SUSANNAH

You should have told me.

CRYSTAL

He said not to worry you. What with the new job and everything. It was all in 'is eyes.

SUSANNAH

His eyes?

CRYSTAL

This rash. All up the side of his 'ead! The ulcers got in his eyes. It was terrible! (*Her eyes glisten at the horror of it.*)

SUSANNAH

My God!

CRYSTAL

Oh, it's okay now.

SUSANNAH

You're sure? I must talk to the doctor ...

CRYSTAL

Nah, honest. He says just to build 'im up ... You know.

SUSANNAH

You should have told me. It's so bloody unfair! He's worked so hard!

CRYSTAL

Will he get 'is job back?

SUSANNAH

Oh yes. He's established. But he's missing this marvellous new project. It's a follow-on from what we were doing here at the Centre. D'you remember? We were telling you about it.

CRYSTAL

Oh. Yeah.

SUSANNAH

I wish you'd go down there, Crystal. The girls would love to hear about hairdressing. You know, just to tell them what it's like. Nothing formal. Just a gossip.

ACT ONE

I could give them a ring if you like. What nights are you free?

CRYSTAL

I work late quite a bit.

SUSANNAH

What about next Thursday? They all come for the disco.

CRYSTAL

No, not really.

SUSANNAH

It's 'for the community.'

CRYSTAL

No, well...

SUSANNAH

I don't want to force you.

CRYSTAL

You know how it is.

SUSANNAH

Sure.

CRYSTAL

Only, I'm on my feet all day.

SUSANNAH

No, I understand, really. It was just that...

CRYSTAL

Oh, sure. I'll get 'is dinner.

She exits.

SUSANNAH crosses to FRANK and takes off his headphones.

                    SUSANNAH

Okay, love?

                    FRANK

Come here.

They embrace.

                    FRANK

I've missed you.

                    SUSANNAH

How's it been?

                    FRANK

Okay.

                    SUSANNAH

No, really...

He gives her a funny little mirthless smile that doesn't convince her.

                    SUSANNAH

God, I should be here!

                    FRANK

You're keeping things going.

                    SUSANNAH

Yes. Birmingham needs you! How long do you think it will be before...?

                    FRANK

(*Quick*) Hard to say.

                    SUSANNAH

But you're feeling better?

                    FRANK

Yuh. Well... more real.

ACT ONE

SUSANNAH

Great. Wait till you see the new schedules. We have not been idle! (*She delves into her bag.*) I brought you some of that ginseng ... Vitamin E ... Clare made some sesame cakes, but the dog with the complicated psyche ate them. God, my mother turned up. She's into haute classe gardening now. Peonies. Are you feeling all right?

FRANK

Mmm.

SUSANNAH

No more panics?

FRANK

A bit. Coping. (*He gives her a darting, accusing look.*) I was bloody glad to get out – I can tell you that.

SUSANNAH

But I thought ... I thought you liked it.

He looks up at the ceiling with a grimace of distaste.

SUSANNAH

(*Slight pause.*) Yes. Not funny. Still, we were lucky ... getting you into Ian's group.

He nods briefly.

SUSANNAH

Look, I know you hated jumping the queue. (*Slight pause.*) What could I do? You were going up the wall! The only alternative was to ...

FRANK

I couldn't have stood ...

SUSANNAH

I know. We've seen it. (*With a little shudder*) Knowing too much makes it tough. Anyway, Ian's a marvellous guy.

FRANK

Yeah. (*Another darting look, unobserved by SUSANNAH*)

SUSANNAH

Human.

FRANK

Mmm.

SUSANNAH

There should be thousands of small units like that. Places where you can work things out without hassle, instead of awful great wards full of ...

FRANK

Yup.

A silence.

SUSANNAH

How goes it with Crystal?

FRANK

Crystal? Oh, fine.

SUSANNAH

Not too ... She doesn't bug you?

FRANK

No, no ... she really looks after me. She's great.

SUSANNAH

Good! Of course, it works on a bilateral level.

ACT ONE

FRANK

What?

SUSANNAH

It's not a patronizing situation. She's able to contribute. There's no question of tenure. I mean, when I get back ...

FRANK

When are you coming?

SUSANNAH

Tomorrow! (*She hugs him fiercely.*) I wish it was tomorrow! Don't worry. I'm not about to abandon the fort. I know the last thing you need is some soppy, individualistic gesture. Hang on, Snoopy! We'll sort Crystal out. For God's sake, she can afford an economic rent – fair rent anyway. She pulls a fortune crimping. I asked her to go down to the Centre, talk to the kids.

FRANK

What did she say?

SUSANNAH

Nothing in it for her. She's pretty single-minded really. After some upmarket guy in a sports car. You can understand it. Her background's pretty deprived. Still, I mean – they are her own sort.

FRANK

She's okay.

SUSANNAH

Oh, great. I was afraid she might be getting on your nerves. She comes on a bit. Still, fine for now. We're lucky really. It bridges the gap.

CRYSTAL enters with a tray of food.

> CRYSTAL
>
> (*To FRANK*) I done you some supper and you got to eat it. (*To SUSANNAH*) You didn't want nothing, did you, love?

> SUSANNAH
>
> (*With swift appraisal of FRANK'S tray*): No thanks. (*To FRANK, in surprise*) Are you eating meat?

> CRYSTAL
>
> Oh, I got him off that vegetarian – it's useless! You can get deficiencies. I read it. You have to eat pounds of chickpeas to get the protein. Unless you're doing heavy labour you can't work off the starch. It's a load of rubbish. D'you want some sauce, Frank?

> FRANK
>
> Thanks.

He sloshes on the sauce and begins to eat heartily, to SUSANNAH's astonishment.

> CRYSTAL
>
> I'll get the crumble. Sure you don't want none, Susannah?

SUSANNAH smiles, shakes her head.

CRYSTAL goes.

> SUSANNAH
>
> Darling. I can shove it all in my Evening Standard, she'll never know.

> FRANK
>
> (*Mouth full*) It's fine, thanks.

ACT ONE

SUSANNAH

You should be on a decent diet. That's dried potato.

He offers her a forkful. She shakes her head, smiling.

SUSANNAH

Oh, I don't care what it is. It's great to see you eating again.

She grasps his hand. He is busy eating.

CRYSTAL enters.

She puts down the pudding, and sets FRANK's napkin straight. FRANK looks up at her and grins.

SUSANNAH

Are you still on antibiotics?

CRYSTAL

His bum's like a pin-cushion.

She gets a look from FRANK.

He bends to the plate, eating.

SUSANNAH

He ought to be on goat's milk yoghurt. It puts flora back in the stomach.

CRYSTAL

I'll get him some cream.

She goes out.

SUSANNAH

(*Embraces him*) Have you missed me?

FRANK

Mmm.

SUSANNAH

If it weren't for this bloody project! Oh! Your hands!

FRANK

What's the matter?

SUSANNAH

They're so thin!

She takes his dinner plate, and fondles his hands.

He lies back among the cushions.

SUSANNAH

You're getting better. I can feel it. There's so much to do. If you could see the kids! I was in tears the other day ... tears of rage. I had to talk to this pisser of a headmaster about this kid. He wants to be a doctor. He's bright, for God's sake, but a West Indian ... not even a Paki. Well, I mean, Christ, no wonder we fragment! Oh, my love. But we grow. It's painful – the mould cracks all the time – it makes us invalids – but we do reshape. We do grow! Did I tell you? We've got twenty-five per cent coloureds in the group now!

CRYSTAL enters, bearing the cream. She's wearing a beautiful, semi-see-through kimono in fragile silk, with floating wisps and panels.

CRYSTAL

Here, Susannah, what d'you think of this?

SUSANNAH

Wow ... Great, man!

CRYSTAL

Got it off a client.

ACT ONE

SUSANNAH

Fantastic. Is it ... um ... is it for anyone special?

CRYSTAL

Nah. I'm breaking it in on Frank. Bit of skin therapy.

She laughs loudly and begins to walk about, showing off the kimono, doing a turn.

SUSANNAH

(*To Frank*) You're not tired?

FRANK

I'm fine.

CRYSTAL

Guess who this is.

SUSANNAH

Raquel Welch?

CRYSTAL

Nah.

SUSANNAH

Marlene?

CRYSTAL

No! Come on, Frank.

FRANK

Marilyn Monroe.

CRYSTAL

Right! Your favourite!

SUSANNAH

Marilyn Monroe?

CRYSTAL

Right. He's been holding out on you, Susannah.

She puts on some music and begins to move to the music.

>SUSANNAH

Do you really go for her?

>FRANK

What, love?

>SUSANNAH

Marilyn Monroe.

>FRANK
>(*Watching CRYSTAL*) Why not?

>SUSANNAH

No reason. You and a few million other guys.

Slight pause. They watch CRYSTAL.

>SUSANNAH

She was such a sad woman.

>FRANK

Oh, I don't know.

Slight pause. They watch CRYSTAL.

>SUSANNAH

What do you mean?

>FRANK

What?

>SUSANNAH

Nothing.

CRYSTAL dances. She is beautiful.

FRANK watches, a dazed expression on his face.

SUSANNAH watches with a smile, wagging her head to the music.

The MUSIC ends.

ACT ONE

CRYSTAL throws herself down, her legs in the air. FRANK does a slow clap, then applauds.

> CRYSTAL
>
> Phew! Wow! Rrrah! Hey! I nearly forgot, Frank. The surprise. We forgot! Susannah's present!

She trips off in her mod shoes to the kitchen.

> SUSANNAH
>
> For me?

> CRYSTAL
>
> Hang on, won't be a sec!

> SUSANNAH
>
> She's great, isn't she?

> FRANK
>
> Yeah.

> CRYSTAL
>
> (*Offstage*) Oh, sod it!

> SUSANNAH
>
> Never mind, Crystal. Next time will do if you can't find it.

> CRYSTAL
>
> (*As she enters*) I'm getting it all over me. Here. For you.

> SUSANNAH
>
> What is it?

> CRYSTAL
>
> Lemon curd. We made it. Frank said you liked it.

> SUSANNAH
>
> Oh, lovely! Oh ... (*She smiles, happy, at FRANK*)

CRYSTAL
Here, 'ave a taste.

She takes back the jar, unscrews the lid, dips a finger in and tastes.

CRYSTAL
Ooh it's great. Here. No, go on ...

They all dip in.

CRYSTAL
(*To FRANK*) You twot. You've got it all over the bed.
Oh, fantastic. Now 'e's got it in 'is hair. Honest – you
should have seen 'im in the kitchen, Susannah,
Jesus!

She laughs and leans over the bed, cleaning him off.

CRYSTAL
'Ere, Susannah – wanna lick it off?

SUSANNAH
Do you need a tissue?

CRYSTAL takes the tissue from her, and dabs at FRANK. The tissue sticks to his hair.

CRYSTAL
(*Giggling*) Now he looks really pretty! Don't 'e look a
pretty boy? You gotta stay like that, eh Susannah?

SUSANNAH
It's very good, Crystal. Is it your own recipe?

CRYSTAL
Me Mum's. It would 'ave been even better only
someone was demandin' onion soup at the time, so it
tastes a bit of onions.

ACT ONE

SUSANNAH

No, it's lovely.

CRYSTAL

All the real thing.

FRANK

Sugar, lemons...

CRYSTAL

Butter and eggs. See? We'll get 'im doing it yet!

SUSANNAH tightens the lid carefully, wraps the jar in a scarf, and puts it carefully into her shoulder bag.

SUSANNAH

Shit, I must go. (*She looks at FRANK poignantly.*)

CRYSTAL

Oh, right. I'll just go and...

She leaves.

SUSANNAH

(*Slight pause.*) I hate leaving you. I hate it. It doesn't feel right. Are you really okay?

He nods briefly.

SUSANNAH

You're sure? (*She bends and kisses him, and then hugs him urgently.*) This thing is really fantastic, love. If it works – and it's bloody going to after all our struggle – we'll stream the pilot and introduce a play-integrated growth scheme for every school-leaver in the UK. Urban, rural, the lot. Believe it, love. Just hang in there, hmm? (*She bends and kisses him on the mouth. Then squeezes his hand in a last affectionate gesture and rises. She gives a clenched fist salute in farewell.)* Up the revolution!

FRANK looks up at her and nods.

> CRYSTAL
>
> (*Offstage*) Oh, you off?
>
> SUSANNAH
>
> (*Going*) I must go. Keep an eye on him for me, Crystal.
>
> CRYSTAL
>
> (*Offstage*) Sure.
>
> SUSANNAH
>
> (*Offstage*) Look, you will give me a call if ... you know, if anything ...
>
> CRYSTAL
>
> (*Offstage*) Yeah, course I will.
>
> SUSANNAH
>
> (*Offstage*) He's lost so much weight!
>
> CRYSTAL
>
> (*Offstage*) Don't worry. Soon build 'im up.

Their voices become distant. The SOUND OF A DOOR CLOSING, sonorous.

CRYSTAL enters.

She crosses to the window, and parts the curtains slightly to watch SUSANNAH recede across the street.

She turns as FRANK looks up. He looks away.

> CRYSTAL
>
> Feeling bad?

ACT ONE

> **FRANK**
>
> No, I feel fine.
>
> **CRYSTAL**
>
> Good.

She sits on the bed.

He stares ahead, his mind elsewhere. She slips a look at him.

Then she jumps up.

> **CRYSTAL**
>
> Ahh! I'm such a bozo!

She runs over to the table and picks up a LARGE ENVELOPE.

She returns and showers TRAVEL BROCHURES over the bed.

> **CRYSTAL**
>
> Right! What do you fancy? Club Mediterranée? It's a new idea. You get to meet people. Nah, maybe not this time. (*She forages.*) What about the Costa del Sol? Warm there. Friend of mine works in a bar near Estepona. In the winter, she goes skiing. Yeah, in Spain! She says it's only a two-hour drive. They're really going to open it up. Bring in facilities.

FRANK laughs briefly.

> **CRYSTAL**
>
> Good for you. Muscles! (*She looks at other brochures.*) What about the Canary Islands?

He looks at her. She smooths his hair back.

> **CRYSTAL**
>
> Think about nice things.

He nods.

CRYSTAL
Why not? You may as well.

She sings and rises. And does a march to the song.

CRYSTAL
'What's the use of worryin' –
It never was worthwhile.
So, pack up your troubles in your old kitbag,
and smile, smile, smile'
(*She salutes at the end of the song.*) My Uncle Ted
used to sing that to me when I were little. Course, he
really went for the Dorsey Brothers and Glenn Miller.
You know, swing. (*Slight pause*) Come on. (*Slight pause*) My trouble is I talk too much.

She sits on the bed again, and nestles close.

CRYSTAL
Fancy a tongue sandwich?

FRANK grabs her with a sudden, urgent savagery. They embrace so fiercely, they roll on to the floor. She hooks her knees round him in a fierce, prolonged hug.

They break apart.

FRANK
What's the matter?

CRYSTAL
Nothing.

FRANK
What are you thinking?

ACT ONE

CRYSTAL

Nothing. You got a bit of colour in your face, that's all.

The lights begin to fade.

They stay on the floor, their arms around each other.

CRYSTAL

Course there's always Jersey. That's nice in the summer. Or Capri. What about Capri?

Fade to black.

ACT ONE - SCENE TWO.

The same.

A few changes. The bed has gone. There is a sofa, some cane furniture, bright cushions, a mobile, and a carrycot.

The pictures have been changed. Mao and Ché have gone, replaced by Aristide Bruant, and a Mucha poster of a girl.

SUSANNAH is onstage. She wears a coat, her bag over her shoulder. She prowls, inspecting the room. She sees a wedding photograph on a bookcase, crosses, picks it up, and looks at it intently.

CRYSTAL

(*Offstage*) Won't be a minute. I'll just turn the oven down.

CRYSTAL enters, bright in a Laura Ashley dress and a Twiggy bandeau.

CRYSTAL

Oh, don't look at that. We was all pissed out of our 'eads.

SUSANNAH replaces the photograph carefully.

>   SUSANNAH
> You look wonderful.

>   CRYSTAL
> Yeah. Not too bad. Cost a fortune that. I was thinkin' of 'avin' it dyed, so I could wear it round the clubs.

>   SUSANNAH
> So ... how've you been?

SUSANNAH shrugs.

>   CRYSTAL
> Sit yerself down. Take your coat off. 'Ere, I'll 'ang it up for you.

>   SUSANNAH
> Don't bother.

>   CRYSTAL
> No, it's no trouble.

>   SUSANNAH
> Thank you.

>   CRYSTAL
> You look ever so well.

>   SUSANNAH
> Thanks. (*She sits.*)

>   CRYSTAL
> Frank's not back. Any minute. Would you like a drink? I don't know what we've got ...

It is all sitting ready on a drinks trolley.

>   CRYSTAL
> Whisky? Gin, vodka? Bacardi?

ACT ONE

SUSANNAH

Oh ... ah, I'll ...

CRYSTAL

How about a sherry?

SUSANNAH

Fine

CRYSTAL

Light or dark?

SUSANNAH

What? Oh, light.

CRYSTAL

It's more dry. The light.

SUSANNAH

Yes.

She watches as CRYSTAL pours the sherry carefully into the correct glass, then pours herself a generous whisky.

CRYSTAL

It's been ages. You didn't mind me ringing ... ?

SUSANNAH

Of course not.

CRYSTAL

Only, we met some of his friends, and they said, like, you was back. It seemed silly not to. Well, you know, you're all friends, and we often have little do's. Anyway, I said: 'listen, I'm gonna ring Susannah.'

SUSANNAH

What did he say?

CRYSTAL

Huh! Don't listen to 'im. No, it's really nice. Cheers.

They drink. Slight pause.

CRYSTAL

I'm glad you could come.

SUSANNAH

You're looking very well.

CRYSTAL

Put on a bit of weight.

SUSANNAH

It doesn't show.

CRYSTAL

I still have to suck in. (*She draws herself in.*) Come and see Nicole.

They exit. We hear their voices.

CRYSTAL

(*Offstage*) There! What do you think of her? ... Ah, she's asleep ... Ah! Who do you think she looks like? Look, a little bubble! Did you see? Mum made the jacket. It's wool. Most of the stuff I got's acrylic. It's better for washing, but wool's warmer really. Look at 'er little fist! She always does that. D'you like the blue elephant? My sister-in-law gave it me. I said it should have been pink. Ooh, now don't wake up, there's a good girl. P'raps we'd better ...

Enter SUSANNAH and CRYSTAL

SUSANNAH

Are you feeding her yourself?

ACT ONE

CRYSTAL

I did at first. Hey, it makes you ever so tired. Anyway, I'm back at work now, so she's on the bottle. It's better really. You're more free.

SUSANNAH

You manage all right?

CRYSTAL

Oh yes. I drop her in the nursery. I'm dead lucky – it's only down the road. Then, pick 'er up at four, do the shopping, get back in time for Frank's tea. It works very well really.

Silence.

SUSANNAH

She's lovely.

CRYSTAL

Ah, she's no trouble. I like babies. Well, they're cuddly, ain't they? Even if you do 'ave to clean up the shit! So ... how've you been? Still workin' wiv the ... what was it you was doin' ... wiv the kids?

SUSANNAH

Oh – no, that's finished. There was a change of authority.

CRYSTAL

Wotta shame.

SUSANNAH

Yes.

CRYSTAL

Didn't you do that panto thing? That show you was into?

SUSANNAH

No, well, actually, we did a smaller piece. A sort of goodbye thing.

CRYSTAL

Nice. What was it about?

SUSANNAH

We tried to improvise on things the kids brought themselves. We were anxious not to impose.

CRYSTAL nods wisely.

SUSANNAH

Obviously, the idea was to celebrate *their* feelings, *their* values.

CRYSTAL

Sort of, do your own thing sort of thing?

SUSANNAH

(*Delighted*). Exactly!

CRYSTAL

What did they choose? (*With a laugh.*) Horror comics?

SUSANNAH

I know! Actually, we did a thing on canals.

CRYSTAL

Canals?

SUSANNAH

We got them going round the libraries, researching the records. You know, old maps, books, songs ... The singing was great. (*She sings*)
If thou'll plod me,
Then I'll plod thee,
And the horse'll plod the three o' we.

ACT ONE

> The towpath's long,
> But my man is strong,
> And to Pluckett's Lock,
> We'll surely be.

She ends dashingly, and looks to CRYSTAL for a response.

SUSANNAH
With a rock backing, of course.

CRYSTAL
Oh. Yeah. Sure.

SUSANNAH
I brought some pictures. I thought Frank might like to see them.

Silence.

CRYSTAL
I'm sorry you couldn't come to the wedding. We missed you.

SUSANNAH
Yes.

CRYSTAL
If it wasn't for you, we wouldn't have met. I mean, it's not as if you and Frank was serious.

SUSANNAH
We weren't married, if that's what you mean.

CRYSTAL
He said you didn't want to.

SUSANNAH
Oh. Well, he certainly never asked.

CRYSTAL

But you're not into it, your lot. You've jacked all that in. (*Pause*) It was his idea, you know, getting married.

SUSANNAH

You didn't think about an abortion?

CRYSTAL

No! I hate it. I wouldn't! Anyway, I'd be too scared. You can get yourself effed up for good doin' that. 'Appened to a friend of mine. Anyway ...

SUSANNAH looks at her. CRYSTAL shrugs.

CRYSTAL

Look, he'd already asked me by then. We was goin' to get married. That's why I never bothered. We was well away when you came down to see us that time. It was a bit awkward really.

SUSANNAH

I didn't know that.

CRYSTAL

No, well, he should 'ave said. Still, he was ill. I think he didn't want to upset you.

SUSANNAH

Upset me!

CRYSTAL

He was feeling bad about leaving all the work to you.

SUSANNAH

Why didn't he tell me? He could have said something! For God's sake! We'd been together for five years!

CRYSTAL

But you was never serious.

ACT ONE

SUSANNAH

Serious? What's that supposed to mean? I'm sorry but – look, this was my home! I found it! God knows it took long enough. I even plastered the walls. When I found this flat, there was one cold tap sticking out of the wall – over there. That was it! I can't believe it's the same place. I'm sorry, Crystal, I don't want to be rude. It's just that everything looks so different.

CRYSTAL

(*Small*) Well, it's bound to be, innit? (*Slight pause*) Frank's changed.

SUSANNAH

Changed? What do you mean? Is he all right?

CRYSTAL

Oh yes, but he's given up all that. Well, you know.

SUSANNAH

All what?

CRYSTAL

All that stuff.

SUSANNAH

What do you mean? What stuff?

CRYSTAL

You know – projects. What you were doin' together. He's settlin' down, Susannah.

SUSANNAH

Frank? Settling down? (*She gives a short laugh.*) He's vulnerable. He always has been. Used to faint when we visited loony bins. It gets the men. No, not Frank. He's a fighter. Look ... Crystal. I'm not trying to ... Look, believe me. It's just that Frank's very special. Not just to me. Well, to me as well ... After all, we were together for a ... (*She falters*) ... for a long time. Naturally it was a blow. It was a shock. You must have realized that, both of you. How could I have come down? I'm surprised you even thought of asking. Couldn't believe it. To be honest, I still can't. Then, when I heard about the baby, there wasn't much point. (*She sighs.*) Was he hurt? That I didn't come to the wedding?

CRYSTAL

I think he was relieved, really. You know what they're like.

SUSANNAH

Anyway, there it is. And, after all, five years of me and he ends up in the bin.

CRYSTAL

Nah, it weren't that. It was overwork!

SUSANNAH

Yes. Yes, he did risk himself. We all did. A lot of it ... okay, a bit half-arsed ... but at least some of it will stick! You have to try. It's not going to work any more, running for the same old burrows. We're rafting off into space. God! Frank sees it. He said to me one day: 'Suze ... you know what's going to do for us all? Not the failure of intellect, moral muscle – but the failure of imagination! They're all too busy with their snouts in the trough to smell the fire.'

CRYSTAL

Yeah, he says some really daft things.

ACT ONE

SUSANNAH

And she was ... real?

FRANK

Something like that.

SUSANNAH

Oh, come on! Look ... I know it cracked for you. God knows you ... But, Frank ... (*She takes a turn*) What do you mean? Aren't high-rises real? Aren't the kids we work with real? For God's sake, weren't we real?

FRANK

No, not really. I don't think so.

SUSANNAH

Not real? All that work? All that fucking we did? Not real?

FRANK

It was different.

SUSANNAH

(*After a pause*) What you mean is: you've given up. Caved in.

FRANK

I don't know. Perhaps.

SUSANNAH

Well, I do. I felt it coming. Long before the breakdown. Manic! Social guilt! Idiotic! The rest of us couldn't even see a movie! Remember the night you found me reading Maigret? Your face! I thought you were going to knife me. (*Slight pause*) Ian told me it would end up in suicide or a crack-up ...

FRANK

He said that?

CRYSTAL appears in the doorway, in an apron.

SUSANNAH

He said it to you!

CRYSTAL

Chicken soup?

SUSANNAH

You wouldn't listen!

CRYSTAL

It's ready.

They wave at her vaguely.

SUSANNAH

We trusted you. Stuck our necks out.

CRYSTAL

Where shall we ...

SUSANNAH

Serves us right. (*To CRYSTAL*) Nothing but bloody, bourgeois, individualist adventurism.

CRYSTAL

Eh?

SUSANNAH

The guru! (*Waving a hand at him.*)

CRYSTAL gives him a blanched look and disappears.

SUSANNAH

You should have gone for a Jesus cult. You'd be king of the ashram by now.

ACT ONE

SUSANNAH

He'll never give up. I know that. That is one thing I know for certain. You're obviously what he needs. If it's working for him. Just so long as he's on his base again. Got his head back. I couldn't ... but there's no danger of that. Not Frank. How is he, in himself?

CRYSTAL

He's fine. I mean, 'e's different. My muvver says 'e's a changed man.

SUSANNAH

How?

CRYSTAL

Drop more?

SUSANNAH shakes her head.

CRYSTAL

Sure? We've got plenty.

SUSANNAH

No thanks.

CRYSTAL

I'll just freshen mine up.

She crosses and helps herself liberally to more whisky.

CRYSTAL

He's settled down. (*She helps herself to ice.*) Well, bound to – with the kiddie, and all.

SUSANNAH

Yes.

CRYSTAL

He's gettin' on ever so well at the school. He likes teaching. I mean, we don't go out much. We're savin' up. I can't wait to get a place of me own. A proper house, you know, wiv a garden.

SUSANNAH

Does he see any of his friends?

CRYSTAL

Oh yes. Now and then. We've joined the Labour Party. Well, it was to please my Dad, really.

SUSANNAH

(*Shocked*) You what?

CRYSTAL

The Labour Party. We go down there for a drink every Friday.

SUZANNAH

Oh God.

CRYSTAL

What's the matter? Don't you approve?

SUSANNAH

Of Social Democracy? My God. Well, that's it.

She gets up, and picks up her bag.

CRYSTAL

You off?

SUSANNAH

Yes, I'm sorry. There's no ...

ACT ONE

CRYSTAL

But I've got a steak and kidney in the oven. What's the matter? Susannah ... (*A wail, as she bursts into tears.*)

SUSANNAH

Oh love. Oh ... Tch! Sit down ...

She cuddles CRYSTAL who weeps.

SUSANNAH

Don't cry. Oh, my dear. All right, you cry. Have a good cry.

CRYSTAL

I've been a bit tired lately. What with working and the baby ... He's late!

SUSANNAH

Bastard was always late. Hang on, I've got a hankie somewhere.

CRYSTAL

He promised he'd be back on time.

SUSANNAH

Would you like another drink?

There is a sound at the door. They both turn.

FRANK is standing there.

CRYSTAL

(*Voice quivering*) You're late!

FRANK

What's the matter?

CRYSTAL runs out of the room, weeping.

FRANK

What's up?

SUSANNAH

I seem to have upset her.

He turns away, takes off his coat, and puts down his stuff.

SUSANNAH

I hear you've joined the Labour Party.

FRANK exits to see CRYSTAL.

He returns almost at once.

SUSANNAH

Is she all right?

FRANK

Yes.

SUSANNAH

I shouldn't have come of course.

FRANK

Why not?

SUSANNAH

Although, it's probably more organic. Or isn't that the in word anymore?

FRANK

I don't know.

SUSANNAH

Well, since I am here, you might as well fill me in. Like, why you did it.

He doesn't answer.

Pause.

FRANK

I had to.

SUSANNAH

What do you mean?

FRANK

I had to, that's all.

SUSANNAH

Because she was pregnant?

FRANK

(*After a pause.*) Ye-es.

SUSANNAH

You bloody liar. She told me you asked her to marry you before that. You hateful, sodding liar. (*Slight pause*) Christ.

Pause.

FRANK

I don't know. (*Pause*) She was there when I needed someone.

SUSANNAH

You had me.

FRANK

That was different. (*Slight pause*) Different world.

SUSANNAH

Our world.

FRANK

(*Frowns*) Yes. (*Pause*) It wasn't real. It was all out there. Unreal.

ACT ONE

SUSANNAH
Was it the breakdown?

He looks nervous that CRYSTAL might hear.

SUSANNAH
Well what? Some sort of gesture? Direct-action consciousness raising? Or did you just fall for nursey?

FRANK
Susannah. (*He gestures for her to keep her voice down.*)

SUSANNAH
I want to know!

FRANK
Look, will you ...

SUSANNAH
I want to know, dammit! (*She walks about, angry.*) You didn't even get in touch! When I tried to ring, all I got was her on the line rabbiting on about a white wedding. She even asked me to be a bloody bridesmaid – did you know that?

FRANK
No, of course not.

SUSANNAH
I'm not talking about her, I'm talking about *you*. Why? Why didn't you ring? I mean, you must have ... What did you think? Didn't you think about me? You must have thought *something*. Unless you were round the bloody twist. I'm sorry. But why? Just tell me why? You owe me. I want to know why.

ACT ONE

FRANK

Oh, stop it.

SUSANNAH

Well what do you know? What have you ever known? You're privileged.

FRANK

Me?

SUSANNAH

Yes, you! You've never been off the tit. Eleven-plus, scholarship, research fellowship, project grant. You're free ... white ... and male. And you've caved in.

Pause.

FRANK

I'm sorry. I wish I could ... (*He sighs deeply and rubs his head.*) The fact is, I'm tired. I've been teaching all week. My brain's a mush.

SUSANNAH

(*Slight pause*) And the rest of us don't work, I suppose.

Another slight pause.

FRANK

What are you doing now?

SUSANNAH

I'm with Brian Mason. New set-up. Kids in care. Not more than eight kids to a house. At least the numbers are possible.

FRANK

Sounds good.

SUSANNAH

Except that I've just been promoted. At the moment it's eight little pairs of accusing eyes. God, just when they were beginning to trust me! (*Slight pause*) Where are you teaching?

FRANK

Compton Beck

SUSANNAH

What? My God. Middle-class! My God. Three years we worked to get that project off the round. Fighting the bloody government, the GLC, Nuffield, Arts Council, Rowntree ... Keep going till they crumble, remember? And then you cop out. And bring the rest of us down with you. A breakdown, yes. But you never came back!

Silence.

He moves about the room. He pauses by the table and picks up a book. He turns the pages idly.

FRANK

I read to her. In the evenings. (*He puts the book down.*) It died on me. All of it. All the collaborative, collective crap of it. And the polemic. Yes, the polemic we were peddling ...

SUSANNAH

What's wrong with that? Group decision! Raise consciousness among the cases. Fight submissiveness ...

FRANK

So, we indoctrinated. Oh, we weren't into fascism. There weren't any slogans or uniforms. No giveaways.

ACT ONE

'Hi kids, I'm Frank, this is Susie, what say we all sit in a circle? And straight into the knocking copy.

SUSANNAH

I don't recall you with a better suggestion. On the contrary ...

FRANK

Banging away at the pit-props with fraternal smiles. Oh, we were going to clear the lot away. Revolution. Fresh start ...

SUSANNAH

You believed it.

FRANK

(*Smiles at her*) The humanist dream.

SUSANNAH

Yes!

FRANK

Only without blood, of course. Messy stuff, that.

SUSANNAH

Right. Damn right. Our way. The possible way. Words – media – subversion.

FRANK

Subversion? Subversion ... us? Susannah, we're the bloody props!

SUSANNAH

What?

FRANK

Destroy the system ... our sort? We cultivate it. 'Inter-Related Structures of Third World Matrix Performances. Foreword by Professor Schumberg,

Cal Tech.' Whatever it is we nourish, it isn't the oppressed. When we arrive, when we knock on all those doors, the tension goes up!

SUSANNAH

Balls. Who brought every resident on the Churchill Estate out on the street?

FRANK

Was anything done? (*Slight pause*) We're social workers. It's us and Valium instead of a housing policy. We got rid of the nuclear family all right – for you and bloody Brian Mason to go and play mothers and fathers with the debris. Till it's time to make the right career choice and move on.

SUSANNAH

I can't believe this. Industrialized society got rid of the extended family. We, the robot consumers, exist to man the machines. I quote you.

FRANK

Oh? So, let us not impose ourselves. Gahd, we're not into hierarchy. Boss figures? Us? As though we aren't imposing ourselves just by being there! What the hell are we doing, crashing into people's lives?

SUSANNAH

I'm not listening to this. It's sick.

FRANK

(*Shouting*) We add to the pain! We're one more threat!

CRYSTAL erupts into the room, indignant.

CRYSTAL

Look, d'you mind? You'll wake the baby!

ACT ONE

SUSANNAH

Oh ... God – sorry love. No, don't go.

FRANK

Stay, Crystal. Don't go.

CRYSTAL sits on the edge of the sofa. Silence.

SUSANNAH

(*Mutters*) I refuse to accept them and us. I never have. It's your problem. (*Direct*) I do not detach myself from the human race as you so consistently and fatally do. And please don't correct my grammar. Nobody's pretending it's easy. God knows, there's little enough on offer for most people ...

CRYSTAL

Yeah.

SUSANNAH

What? But if we can break out a few choices. Give them a chance to choose. Make some sort of celebration ...

FRANK

Choose?

CRYSTAL

(*Warning*) Frank ...

FRANK

Choose what? Celebrate what? Flyovers? (*To CRYSTAL*) No, stay!

SUSANNAH

(*To CRYSTAL*) Don't go ...

FRANK

What was it? Yeah, sure – community theatre. The great civic venting operation. Steel bands. Your actual black faces. Way out, man. Only, when they got themselves a carnival together last year, you were all shitting yourselves. It was getting out of hand, right? Or was it that you felt that your delicate white faces weren't all that gratefully welcome? After all . . . (*He directs this at CRYSTAL, who happens to be in front of him*) . . . it is our backyard, right? Robert Ardrey on territory, right?

CRYSTAL grimaces at him to hush up, then exits quickly.

SUSANNAH

Frank, that's so unfair. Okay . . . okay.

FRANK

There's no need to humour me. I'm perfectly all right.

SUSANNAH

I didn't suggest that you weren't. I think you're being unfair, that's all. But if that's what you believe, I'm not claiming to lay down lines. On anything.

FRANK

Sure. I know. The atom is random. We make ourselves up. The old order smasheth. Decadence rules. So what do we have? Here we are, kids. Come and get it. A great big steaming basinful of fucking nothing at all.

SUSANNAH

Frank, I don't know what you're talking about.

FRANK

No, of course you don't. You're bolted up the bloody middle like Frankenstein's monster. Listen. Listen!

ACT ONE

Aren't we people too? We've turned ourselves into fucking computerized case-histories, along with the rest of them. My God! I'm telling you! The more we stepped backwards into that sour-faced vacuum, the more I ... Oh Christ, run for your life! Find it, quick! A world of green forest and wet pools – lakes of white water ... leaves and violet skies ... blue electric toads, hopping ...

SUZANNAH is alarmed.

SUSANNAH
(*Speaking in a careful, level voice*) Frank? What are you talking about?

FRANK
The more 'real' we become, the more I ...

Words fail him. He plays with a lamp fitting, unable to continue.

FRANK
We're parasites.

SUSANNAH
Don't.

FRANK
We suck the life out. It makes us feel good. The pay's shitty, we say. Who can afford a car? Never mind, it's the work that counts.

SUSANNAH
Yes. It is. And what is more, some of us see it as more than bandages. A vehicle for change.

FRANK
Change? Oh, we change things. We're the change-makers all right. We take the magic out of life. And

what do we give them? Who needs books on cows and rabbits? Are they real life? Let's celebrate reality for fuck's sake. Pop-up sex manuals. Jenny and Kevin at the supermarket. Who needs Hans Andersen? Anyway, wasn't he a paedophile? Or was that Lewis Carroll? Dante, Titian – are they the revolution? Rembrandt, Tolstoy? Elitist garbage, man. Culture's for the pooves! Remember your beauty contest? Eight-year-olds in stuffed bras?

SUSANNAH

Yes, you did make your feelings known. May I remind you that, as far as the kids were ...

FRANK

'Kids' ...

SUSANNAH

Yes, kids. What do you want me to call them? Juveniles? They enjoyed themselves. What's wrong with tits, for God's sake? Anyway, look, we agreed! Some diminution in quality – yes! For as long as it takes.

FRANK

We kill people.

SUSANNAH

You're mad.

SUSANNAH

We suck the life out.

SUSANNAH

(*In a singing tone*) I think I hear the cracked bell of revisionism.

ACT ONE

FRANK

Remember going to Austria last year?

SUSANNAH

I asked you to come, you wouldn't take the time off.

FRANK

Once to ski, and again in the spring ... to renew yourself. For the fight. You didn't even bring back pressed flowers. You took pictures, but you didn't show them to the kids. Why not?

SUSANNAH

I don't know!

FRANK

Because it was nothing to do with them. That was *your* life. Anyway, ours not to point up the gap. Bridge-building? Common ground? Skiing? For the likes of black kids in North London? Not on. And don't remind me that your father once worked for the Water Board. Not one act of imaginative love. Not one.

SUSANNAH

You seem, at least, to have your energy back.

FRANK

I've been trying to get it right. (*He sighs deeply*) I don't know what 'it' is anymore.

SUSANNAH

Oh, for God's ...

FRANK

I don't know anything. Except her. (*Pause*) I read to her. In the evenings. We're reading Lord Jim at the moment. Remember the opening, where he goes on about Jim's job as a tout for a ship's chandler?

SUSANNAH

What?

FRANK

After a couple of pages describing the tattiness of a tout's life, he ends up . . . 'a beautiful and humane occupation.' Irony. She liked that. She got it.

Pause.

SUSANNAH

You pompous renegade. You bloody social-democrat do-gooder.

FRANK

It's real. I feel real.

SUSANNAH

Well, good luck to you. (*She picks up her bag.*) What's she like in bed?

FRANK

A goer. I have trouble keeping up.

SUSANNAH

I notice she does all the cooking and shopping – all the work. What's in it for her?

FRANK

She wants a husband, children. She's not after the world.

SUSANNAH

She'd better be, or she'll end up like your Mum and mine. Vicious. You bloody exploitative shit. I hope it rots off.

SUSANNAH leaves.

A short pause.

ACT ONE

CRYSTAL enters in a dressing gown.

CRYSTAL

She gone?

He nods.

CRYSTAL

Jesus.

He doesn't reply. She contemplates him.

CRYSTAL

I had a shower.

FRANK

Oh?

CRYSTAL

Smell me.

FRANK

(*He grabs her and buries his face*) Mmmm ...

CRYSTAL

Guess what it is. No, you got to guess!

FRANK

It's called 'Expensive.'

CRYSTAL

(*Laughing*) You ain't seen nuffing.

She drops the dressing gown. She is wearing very little, but it is sensational.

FRANK

Christ!

CRYSTAL

Thought I'd better do somefing.

FRANK

No need.

CRYSTAL

Really?

FRANK

Look, it's old history.

CRYSTAL

I started to feel like, you know, a fucking gooseberry in me own place.

FRANK

Finished. Over.

CRYSTAL

Right. Well, in that case ... (*She sits on his lap, legs astride.*)

FRANK

Here, what about my dinner?

CRYSTAL

It'll keep. (*She kisses him.*)

FRANK

I'm a hungry man.

CRYSTAL

I know. (*Kisses him.*) I've made allowances. (*Kisses him.*) Last course first tonight.

They embrace.

Lights fade to black.

END OF ACT ONE.

ACT TWO

ACT TWO – SCENE ONE.

The Flat. Ten years later.

The décor is now retro, with Thirties' lamps and some pictures of old movie stars in plastic frames.

There are signs of children. A child's bicycle, toys brimming from a washer-woman's basket.

Apart, there is a large old trestle table with a typewriter, and piles of papers and books, which have spread to nearby furniture. There is a large board, with leaflets tacked up. These, too have spread to the wall. This is FRANK's working area. It is in sharp contrast to the smart sofa, lamps, and the retro side table with the music centre.

FRANK sits at the table, working. He is absorbed in what he is doing – writing an article straight on to the typewriter. He makes errors, and curses under his breath. He reaches behind him, grabs a bottle of beer, drinks, and continues work.

The telephone rings. He grabs it absently.

FRANK

Yup? ... Oh, hullo Ann ... good ... Yeah, I brought them here. We managed to get some transport ... Yeah, right ... Look, don't bother. I'll drop you in a thousand copies in the morning. The sooner we move them ... Yeah. See you.

He puts down the phone and resumes working.

CRYSTAL enters.

She is now a successful West End hairdresser. She looks slender in highly fashionable clothes, with beautifully washed, simple hair, and a model's modulated make-up. Her shoes and bag are expensive.

She carries two bags – one a glossy carrier, the other with food.

> FRANK

That you?

> CRYSTAL

Nah, Brooke Shields. Your lucky night.

She unpacks food and takes it out to the kitchen.

> CRYSTAL

What's the time?

> FRANK

Half past seven.

She returns, takes an expensive-looking dress from the glossy carrier-bag, holds it up against herself briefly for his inspection, and goes, with the dress.

> FRANK

You going out again?

CRYSTAL enters, throwing off her clothes rapidly but without fuss.

> CRYSTAL

What's it look like? Aw, I'm bushed.

She exits.

FRANK gets up, picks up her clothes and takes them out.

> FRANK

(*Returning*) Anything special for the kids? (*He picks up the food carrier, and reads the label.*) Christ!

ACT TWO

CRYSTAL

(*Offstage*) At least I know they're getting some decent nosh. Tell 'em it's in the fridge. Where are they?

FRANK

Next door, watching the film with Inez.

CRYSTAL enters, drying herself, and throwing on clothes.

CRYSTAL

That bloody water's not hot again. Did you ring the plumber?

FRANK claps his hand to his head. He has forgotten.

CRYSTAL

Oh no! I need a bloody shower when I come in. I'm sweating like a pig! (*She grabs the telephone and dials.*)

FRANK

What are you doing?

CRYSTAL

Ringing up for an emergency ...

FRANK

Don't do that! It's thirty quid before they come through the door. I've told you. I've got somebody!

CRYSTAL

Hullo? All-Night Plumbers? ... Yeah, me again ... Yeah, same problem. Could you? ... Good. Right. Hey, hello? ... Could you ring both bells? Yeah. (*She puts down the telephone.*) They'll be here in half an hour.

FRANK

I'm going out. I thought you were going to be in tonight.

CRYSTAL

It's all right. I've told them to ring Inez's bell.

She finishes getting ready. He watches her.

FRANK

You look good.

She blows him a kiss.

FRANK

Where are you off to? Anywhere special?

CRYSTAL

(*Spitting into her eye make-up*) Now, now.

FRANK

What?

CRYSTAL

Listen, love. I don't ask about your things.

FRANK

Sure.

CRYSTAL

(*Doing her mouth*) Just a couple of beers with the mates. You doing a movie?

FRANK

Yeah, thought I might.

CRYSTAL

Which one?

She gives him a quick, speculative look behind his back.

FRANK

Alan Arkin.

ACT TWO

CRYSTAL

Good. You like him. Tell you what. Why don't you look in on Jean and Freddy after?

FRANK

I'll see how I feel.

CRYSTAL

(*As she finishes her toilette with rapid precision and gives him a hug.*) Yeah, go on.

FRANK

(*Not convinced*) Why not?

CRYSTAL

You could eat at that Greek place.

FRANK

Okay.

CRYSTAL

Be nice that.

FRANK

Right. That's me sorted out.

CRYSTAL

Ah, you know what I'm like.

She turns for him to do up the back of her dress. Then she throws her coat over her shoulders, remembers something, totters in her heels to the bag she emptied when changing her bag, finds an envelope, and thrusts it under his nose.

FRANK

What's this?

CRYSTAL

Can't you read? It's the phone bill.

FRANK

(*Reading the amount, whistles*) Christ!

CRYSTAL

(*Checking herself in the mirror*) Yeah. Down to you and your lot.

FRANK

Come on! You're never off the bloody thing.

CRYSTAL

Rubbish. You're 'ere more than me. Why don't you pass the hat round those mates of yours – ripping you off for free calls. I wouldn't stand for it. Ahhh!

FRANK jumps.

FRANK

Now what's wrong?

CRYSTAL

(*Of sofa*) They keep sittin' on it!

FRANK

Who?

CRYSTAL

All those limp dicks of yours!

FRANK

Why not? It's a sofa.

CRYSTAL

There you are! Cigarette burn. Ah, what a shame!

FRANK

Come off...

ACT TWO

CRYSTAL

And this end's all squashed. Tch. (*She plumps up the sofa, muttering.*) Bloody meetings! How can you ask anyone back? It's all crummy! (*She tidies swiftly.*) It's no wonder I want to get out of it.

FRANK

Do you?

CRYSTAL

What?

FRANK

Want to get out of it?

CRYSTAL

Oh, don't be so daft.

FRANK

You brought it up.

CRYSTAL

I need some fun at the end of the day, that's all.

FRANK

So do the kids.

CRYSTAL

What's that supposed to mean?

FRANK

Crystal, we never see you.

CRYSTAL

Don't tell such lies.

FRANK

These last few weeks ...

CRYSTAL

I've told you. We're under-staffed!

FRANK

They miss you.

CRYSTAL

Oh yes. Go on. I'm a rotten mother now.

FRANK

I didn't say that.

CRYSTAL

You can't expect me to stick in every night. I want a bit of fun out of life! I won't have it forever.

FRANK

I'm not trying to stop you ...

CRYSTAL

I earn it – I gotta right to spend it. I'm the one that pays the bills.

FRANK

That's not true.

CRYSTAL

Most of 'em. More than half. Everything in this place is what I bought.

FRANK

Rubbish.

CRYSTAL

I have!

FRANK

Balls.

ACT TWO

CRYSTAL

Thank you. Lovely. Super language coming from a schoolteacher. No wonder they're all hooligans.

FRANK

Oh Christ, your tongue.

CRYSTAL

(*She flares, then changes her mind*) Frank ... don't be like that.

She cuddles him. He kisses her.

The TELEPHONE RINGS.

CRYSTAL

Go on. It'll be for you.

FRANK picks up the phone.

FRANK

Hang on, please ...

He divests himself from CRYSTAL, who picks up her things, prior to going out.

CRYSTAL

Which one is it? (*In an upper-class accent*) Lady Jane? Or the little fat one? You know why she sits and reads all that stuff of yours? It's pathetic really. I'm off. (*She crosses for a perfunctory kiss.*) Listen, that quiche and toffee pudding's for the kids ... (*Jokingly*) ... so keep your thieving mitts off it. (*She kisses him again.*) Ciao, lover.

She is about to go, but changes her mind. She crosses, and takes most of his cigarettes from the packet.

FRANK watches her.

CRYSTAL exits.

Then he remembers the phone in his hand.

FRANK

Hullo ... hullo ... sorry to keep you ... hullo, yes ... speaking ... why? ... No, I don't believe it! Where are you? Where are you speaking from? ... Haha ... no, no, I'm just knocked out that's all. (*Pause. He listens, nodding.*) Oh fine ... fine ... good, you mean you? ... Where are you now? ... No, sure, why not? ... Great! I thought you were in Bolivia ... yeah, okay ... No, just come straight up ... Hey, Susannah ... Hullo? (*But she has gone.*)

He puts down the phone and throws himself down on the sofa, his legs up in the air. He is very affected.

He rises and looks around the room. Then he scrapes his papers together, takes the dirty coffee cups from his table, and pushes odd books under the sofa.

He looks around, moves the furniture slightly, takes a look at himself in the mirror, and exits.

He returns, putting on another shirt, and looks in the mirror.

He exits.

He returns, putting on his original shirt. Puts a record on the record player, low. Then finds glasses and opens a bottle of wine.

FRANK

Chambrez, you devil.

He puts on the radiator, stands back, then spins around to check the room.

ACT TWO

He has his back to SUSANNAH when she appears. He spins back to find her standing in the doorway.

SUSANNAH

The door was open.

FRANK

You were quick.

SUSANNAH

I was just round the corner.

For a second, they regard each other across the room. Then they leap into each other's arms.

He swings her round and they hang on to each other for dear life. She gives a little, sad, animal moan.

Eventually, they pull apart, and both become matter-of-fact in manner.

SUSANNAH

You look older.

FRANK

I am older. You look just the same.

SUSANNAH

I don't know. My skin's a terrible mess.

FRANK

You look fine to me.

SUSANNAH

How is everyone? Crystal?

FRANK

You've just missed her.

SUSANNAH

And the family?

FRANK

Fine. They're with the people next door, watching Alan Ladd.

SUSANNAH

Alan Ladd?

They laugh.

SUSANNAH

Have you had any more ... children?

FRANK

No. Just the two ... Nicky and Pete.

SUSANNAH

How old are they now?

FRANK

Ten and eight ... nearly nine.

SUSANNAH

My God, is it really that long? The last time we met was in Leeds. That awful symposium!

FRANK

(*Together*) The symposium! And once in the Fulham Road.

SUSANNAH

Coming out of the pictures.

FRANK

You were with some Chileans.

SUSANNAH

That's right.

A pause.

ACT TWO

FRANK

So, you're back.

SUSANNAH

I'm back.

FRANK

Back in the oo-old country.

SUSANNAH

As they say.

FRANK

Good. Good. How does it feel?

SUSANNAH

Pretty weird. I'm a bit disorientated.

She prowls, inspecting the room – calm, unsmiling, dignified. She bends to look at a picture.

SUSANNAH

(*Murmurs*) I'd no idea I was so chauvinistic.

FRANK

Land of hope and glory, eh? Bit of a change from the dark sub-continent.

SUSANNAH

Yes. So small! How on earth did we ever do it?

FRANK

Conquer the world, you mean? You're right. Distinctly puzzling.

SUSANNAH

(*Sits*) I got an aeroplane to Paris, then the boat-train. Amazing! It was like coming back to a tiny old ghost-town. Everything looks grey, even the people! Nothing seems to work anymore. Holes in the roads – the clocks tell the wrong time. I went to the Post Office. Four booths shut. Two long queues. One not moving. When it was my turn, I asked for the postal rate to Bolivia. He said he didn't know. I said, you *must* know. He went away and didn't come back! What's happened?

FRANK

Oh, c'est la guerre.

SUSANNAH

When I left, there was confrontation. There was colour.

FRANK

Hah.

SUSANNAH

Where did it go? What happened?

FRANK

The money ran out. It *was* all happening. We *were* getting somewhere. Mrs down-the-road from the shop got on the Council. Real change. Movement. And then the Arabs upped the oil ...

SUSANNAH

And down fell Jack.

FRANK

Oh yes. And out of the thickets they came. The carrot and stick boys. The law and order analysts. The up-you bastards. (*Upper-class voice*) 'There you are, you see? Doesn't do, chaps. Back in the old cage.'

SUSANNAH

I'm so out of touch. You mean ... ?

ACT TWO

FRANK

Yeah. Cold climate. When there's no wage packet or hope of employment ... (*He shrugs.*) Fear works. Put your hand in the fire, you won't do it twice. Ask any circus trainer.

SUSANNAH

What about North Sea Oil? I thought we were all going to float away on it.

FRANK

Sold off. Good capitalism. Talk national – deal international.

SUSANNAH

That's depressing.

FRANK

Mmm. So much for the right to work.

SUSANNAH

Yes. I've been reading the figures. It's ... (*She shakes her head, overcome with shock and indignation.*)

FRANK

(*Slight pause.*) They fished a man out of the canal last week with his toolbox tied to his leg.

SUSANNAH gasps.

FRANK

They call it a shake out. Same old story. Who are you governing for. (*Slight pause*) So, it's feel-good movie time, and Space Invaders.

SUSANNAH

Space Invaders? (*She shakes her head, baffled.*)

FRANK

Yup. Who knows? Perhaps we'll go to sleep for four hundred years, like Spain. Could happen.

He exits to the kitchen.

SUSANNAH

Oh, I doubt that! Not here. Not without a fixed system.

FRANK

(*From the kitchen, getting glasses*) We've always had that!

SUSANNAH

What?

FRANK

(*Entering*) We've always had a fixed system. The fucking shires.

SUSANNAH

(*Groans*) Oh no! Not all over again!

FRANK

Sure thing. Flat 'at, gun under the arm. They're all peddling heating systems during the week, but it's up the M1, and let's play squire at the weekends.

SUSANNAH

The old class nastiness? You mean it?

FRANK

And the new Puritanism.

SUSANNAH

Puritanism?

ACT TWO

FRANK

'Victorian values' is the phrase. If you're poor – jobless – it's your own fault. So ... (*He makes a punching gesture.*)

SUSANNAH

A touch of the Puritans may see us through. A bit of sharing, inconspicuous consumption ... (*She smiles.*)

FRANK hugs he fondly.

FRANK

It's good to see you! (*He gives her a drink.*) Welcome home!

SUSANNAH

To your very best health.

FRANK

To you.

They drink.

SUSANNAH

How's the job?

FRANK

I'm supply teaching at the moment.

SUSANNAH

Are you? I had you all dug in as a senior history master. You look pretty busy. (*She picks up a pamphlet.*)

FRANK

Socialist Combination. I've thrown my lot in. Now that it's highly unfashionable.

They laugh.

SUSANNAH

And what about freedom from party dogma?

FRANK

Ah. Freedom. Plenty of that about. Freedom to sink. To go to hell. Opportunities for boys to train as butlers. I'm not kidding. There was a programme on TV.

SUSANNAH

Jesus! (*Slight pause*) What about women?

FRANK

Unemployment hasn't helped. The scene's changed since you left.

SUSANNAH

Oh, how?

FRANK

More polarized. I'll run you down to Greenham Common.

SUSANNAH

Already been. So, you're active?

FRANK

Full-time from next month.

SUSANNAH

(*Surprised*) You're giving up teaching?

FRANK nods.

SUSANNAH

Completely?

FRANK

(*Nods*) I'll miss it.

ACT TWO

SUSANNAH

Can you afford to?

FRANK

Just about. (*He shrugs.*) Crystal pulls a fortune.

SUSANNAH

I see. (*Pause*) Is it okay? You and Crystal?

FRANK

No. But there are the children.

SUSANNAH

Wouldn't they be better off?

FRANK

Possibly. I doubt it. They're all still a bit young. Can I fill you up?

SUSANNAH

Mm, please. It's good. Luxury. I'm used to something much rougher.

FRANK

Yes! What about you? What have you been doing?

SUSANNAH

Working in a mining town.

FRANK

Same place.

SUSANNAH

Most of the time. (*She drinks.*)

FRANK

Well? What's it like? (*He leans forward, eager.*)

SUSANNAH

Oh. (*Slight pause*) Very high up. Very wet. Very cold. Not a bit picturesque.

FRANK

What were you doing there? Martin Raven said he'd heard from you, but that was ages ago.

SUSANNAH

Not much point in writing. I was too tired most of the time. Nothing really, Frank. (*She looks at him bleakly.*) No quaint costumes worth a television team. (*Shrugs*) Just people trying to stay alive.

FRANK

Sounds rough. What were you doing there?

SUSANNAH

Documentation. I was a field officer.

FRANK

Vital.

SUSANNAH

I had to change in '81 ... There was a coup. I've been doing union work.

FRANK

Great!

She turns to look at him, puzzled. Then, she looks around the room, seemingly absorbed in the decorations.

SUSANNAH

(*Absently*) They chew coca leaves. Stops the hunger pangs.

FRANK

You sound bitter.

ACT TWO

SUSANNAH

(*Lightly*) Oh, I am. I am. No one in their right mind would stay there for an hour if there were anywhere else on God's earth. For the last year, I've been counting the days. And it rained for most of them.

FRANK

That bad?

SUSANNAH

(*Short laugh*) Goes for most people on this globe. I sat next to this shit of an American woman on the plane. She was telling me about her villa, near Malaga. All built in the traditional style. Guitar- shaped swimming pool.

He laughs.

SUSANNAH

Only one problem. The Spanish people. So 'dirty.' (*She falters.*)

FRANK

Suze?

SUSANNAH

(*Recovers*) I was talking to one of the miner's wives just before I left. She'd lost another baby. I tried to console her. No, she said. You don't understand. I said I thought I did, but she said no, I couldn't. I was rich. I tried to tell her that I wasn't. That I didn't own a thing. And she looked at me in the eyes. It's a thing they never do, but she was a bit mad from losing the child, and she said: 'You're white. You're rich.'

A pause.

FRANK

You're not going back?

SUSANNAH

I should. I'm experienced. I can just about balance my worth against what I eat. No, I'm not going back. Ever.

Pause.

FRANK

What are you going to do?

SUSANNAH

(*Lightly*) Have a baby, I hope.

FRANK

What? (*Pointing to her stomach in smiling inquiry.*)

SUSANNAH

(*Shakes her head*) No, no. It's just that the only thing I really want to do right now is have a baby. The need to (*exaggerated drawl*) 'give birth' has been rather overwhelming lately. I seem to be somewhat ... seething with it. (*Serious.*) I want a child before I start getting infertile.

FRANK

Is there anyone in mind? I mean ...

SUSANNAH

No.

They look at each other. He laughs.

FRANK

It's fantastically good to see you. Well! Right. So. How are you going to go about it? You going solo?

ACT TWO

SUSANNAH

Possibly. I shall have to find somewhere to live. Acquire an income somehow. I thought teaching. Could you help me with that?

FRANK

Sure.

SUSANNAH

Then there's the father. Have to find myself a feller.

FRANK

What kind of feller?

SUSANNAH

Oh, either a healthy and intelligent one-night stand with intent on my part and innocence on his. Or I could try to set up a more permanent arrangement with a fatherly citizen. Preferably with a roof over his head. God, I'd love my own patch. A few rooms, an apple tree to sit under with my children. You'd be amazed at the things I can do now with a few spuds and an onion. Delicioso.

FRANK

You want to settle down?

SUSANNAH

Probably. It sounds like it.

FRANK

You mean marriage?

SUSANNAH

Possibly.

FRANK

You've changed!

SUSANNAH

Ye-es. No longer the heroine of the revolution.

FRANK

I'm sorry to hear that.

She turns, surprised.

FRANK

They're all on the run now. Following the action. I didn't think you would.

SUSANNAH

It's funny, isn't it? The last time we were here – hah! I remember it...

FRANK

So do I!

SUSANNAH

You seemed to be... I thought you'd... I mean, I really did think you'd...

FRANK

Sold out?

SUSANNAH

I've gone over and over it in my mind. I should have been there. When you were ill. I realize that now.

FRANK

I wasn't myself.

SUSANNAH

I should have been there. That bloody project. God, we were so intense! We were going to change the world! Hah.

ACT TWO

FRANK

I know.

SUSANNAH

I thought we were indissoluble. Mistake number one. We were so in step. At least, that's what I thought. That fucking Pill.

FRANK

What?

SUSANNAH

If it weren't for the Pill, I'd have been pregnant three times over, the way we went at it. Remember the woman downstairs coming up with half the ceiling in her hair? And you offering to show her how it was done? We thought we were so clever. Beating nature. I've been done out of it.

FRANK

Still time.

SUSANNAH

God, the agony of choice! (*She groans.*) I mean! There's never a good time to have a baby. If you can afford it, you're too old. And who needs Marmite sandwiches and little morons for ten years when you're just getting your head together? God, how I envy Crystal!

FRANK

Is that why you've come back? A touch of the domestics?

SUSANNAH

There was a bad mine accident. We lost half the men in the village. Makes you think. About going it alone.

FRANK

Very fashionable now. Single parenting.

SUSANNAH

Is that what they call it? Orphaning children? No.

FRANK

(*Shrugs*) The right to choose.

SUSANNAH

Oh, rights! They need their father. There's a right, if you like. I saw the loss, in the tribe, Imbalance. I've begun to have a silly respect for that rare constant in human psychology – the blood relation.

FRANK

Hah! (*Laughs*) We spent half our time together fending off our bloody parents!

SUSANNAH

Yer ... well, they were squares. Straights. 'Don't show me up, man!'

He laughs and hugs her.

SUSANNAH

Still do anything in the world for us. Who else can you say that of? You couldn't say it of me. I pissed off when you were ill. Your mother didn't. (*She moves away from him, and walks about.*) I want them. My family. Sisters. Aunts. Cousins. Great- uncles once removed. Someone to go to. Argue with. Grumble about. At least they're there! I watched television last night. God, I couldn't believe it! Programme after programme. The Twenties. The Thirties. Bath after bath of nostalgia, all created with such love and affection. What the hell have we done? (*She*

ACT TWO

walks, restless.) I'm tired of being on my own. It's an overrated privilege.

FRANK
You *have* changed.

She laughs.

SUSANNAH
I still talk too much. What about you? What about you, Frank?

FRANK
Here and now? I don't know. Yes. Excited. Pretty excited.

SUSANNAH
(*Her face alight*) You mean ... ?

He turns away.

SUSANNAH
(*She sees he doesn't mean because she's back, and covers quickly.*) Why? What about? About changing your work?

FRANK
Don't know. Can't say. Yes, I suppose it is that. Taking the risk. Only this time it's sane. No more shrieking about revolution – man the fucking barricades. Kids' talk. Murderers' talk. Our aims are as clear as we can make them. Precise. Practical. And modest.

SUSANNAH
Gradualist?

FRANK
Remember what you used to say? Not one hair of a baby's head?

221

SUSANNAH

You gave me shit for it.

FRANK

We have to be realistic. Select. Win where possible. Influence, subvert, create models, communicate. God knows the channels are open now. Anything is possible, d'you see? Because everything's collapsed. Politics. Religion. Imperialism. At least it makes for clarity.

SUSANNAH

Dangerous.

FRANK

Do you think so? I wonder. (*Slight pause*) At least there's less shit. People won't stand for it. No, not anymore. They're a lot more criminal, sure … or, rather, they know where criminality lies. They see the con. I think we could be in with a chance. We're misty, bloody islanders, with a head full of words. Which is a problem …

SUSANNAH

How do you mean?

She leans forward, loving the talk – not able to get enough of it.

FRANK

Romantics, the lot of us. Shakespeare spawn. We could double the gross domestic product if we put turrets on the factories. I've even thought that maybe we should stick with titles. Only not be so mean with it. Spread them around like they did in Russia before the Bolsheviks. Everyone in with a chance for a fur-collared overcoat.

ACT TWO

SUSANNAH

Don't tell me you've become a royalist?

FRANK

Stranger things have happened. (*Slight pause.*) I'm kidding. Under this string vest there beats a pure republican heart.

SUSANNAH

I'm not convinced. You're an Englishman. Quite capable of being corrupted by a piece of shiny ribbon. (*She laughs, and prowls among his papers.*) What's the party line?

FRANK

Anarcho-syndicalist.

SUSANNAH

De-centralization?

FRANK

Community politics. Fifty-fifty ownership, management and labour – government and people. Internationalist. Some ecology. We're eclectic. And pragmatic.

SUSANNAH

Sound like the new ... what is it? Social Democratic Party.

FRANK throws a cushion at her.

FRANK

Marxist hack!

SUSANNAH

And you're happy?

FRANK

Nothing's perfect. I have regular moments of pure fascism.

SUSANNAH

Plus ça change.

FRANK

... and I wish I could make some money. Like my brother.

SUSANNAH

How is he?

FRANK

Weighs fifteen stone and has five children, boxer dog, and a villa in Majorca, mit pool.

SUSANNAH

Nice?

FRANK

Very comfy.

SUSANNAH

Ye-es. Yes ... I want a baby. How about it?

FRANK

You looking at me, squire?

SUSANNAH

You'd do. You'd do very well. In fact ... In fact, it's going to be difficult to find a substitute for you.

FRANK

Suze ...

They kiss gently. He takes her hand.

ACT TWO

SUSANNAH

I saw your daughter. Just after she was born. When I came to see you and we had that flaming row. I remember it very clearly. I wasn't into babies at all and Crystal had her tricked out in pink with obscene rabbits in spats camping about all over the cot.

FRANK

I remember.

SUSANNAH

I really hated being forced in there, and I was determined not to make the usual noises. What I wasn't prepared for was this ... person. She was fast asleep and frowning, as though she was concentrating on something as hard as she could. It was as though she was growing. She had your long skull. I've never forgotten. Are you faithful, you and Crystal?

FRANK

I am. She isn't. She's very good with the children. Natural mother. As they say. We-ell, at the moment it's not so hot. She's stopped feeding us.

SUSANNAH

(*Drily*) Oh dear. Poor old you.

FRANK

Figure of speech.

SUSANNAH

What's gone wrong?

FRANK

She's fed up.

SUSANNAH

With you?

FRANK

Mostly.

SUSANNAH

Why?

FRANK

I don't stand up to her. Not in the way that she wants.

SUSANNAH

Why not? If that's what she needs.

FRANK

Come on. You can't play a part in your own home. Home's where you leave off. (*Slight pause.*) She's restless. She doesn't know it but, what she really wants is a child every other year. That's what her body wants. They're all breeders, the women in her family. Insatiable. She has such a body. Breasts. Contours. Valleys. All ... alive! It's a crime to clothe her. She should be decked with flowers and worshipped. I'm a mere mortal. I deprive her. So she takes it out on me.

SUSANNAH

It sounds disastrous.

FRANK

Yeah. But it's poetry. And the children. I live in a permanent daze of wonder at the beauty of them. The things they say! New! Fresh. Another coinage. They don't see with our eyes. They come after us. They judge us. Of course, at the moment, I'm Dad. I can do

ACT TWO

no wrong. They'll find me out soon enough. Realize I'm not Superman.

SUSANNAH
(*Slight pause*) Frank ... it's bad, isn't it?

FRANK
Yes.

SUSANNAH
Let go.

FRANK
I can't.

SUSANNAH
But surely ...

FRANK
'My Kingdom.'

SUSANNAH
But if it's no good? I could put up a fight this time. I'm much tougher now.

FRANK
No. Not yet, anyway.

SUSANNAH
Oh, for Christ's sake! If you think I'm going to stand back and watch you ... Have you any idea what I've ... (*She catches herself, with difficulty*) I'm sorry. It's your life. But, oh Frank, if you knew how lucky we are. To waste any of it ...! (*Pause*) It's self-indulgent to talk of bringing even one more mouth into the world. We're cannibals, the lot of us. Living off cash crops when we could ... (*She pauses, then turns and speaks mildly.*) We should stop. Here. Right now. This

minute. All of us. Most of the volume of pain in the world could be easily prevented. We have the means. (*She sighs.*) I escaped. Because I could. Every night I'd crawl into my damp, sagging hammock and dream about clean, dry clothes, about red meat ... beef, chops, liver. About lights that switched on. Warmth. About cars, buses, smooth roads, shops, theatres, libraries. All the things I could have again, and that they would never, ever have.

FRANK

Love ... (*He puts an arm around her.*)

SUSANNAH

The woman on the plane showed me her new handbag. Crocodile. A thousand dollars. And she was proud of it. Enough to feed a village for a year.

FRANK

Yes. Yes, a bit of a joke.

SUSANNAH

(*Pause*) I don't know what to do. Except, as I say ...

Slight pause.

FRANK

Join us. (*He indicates the poster on the wall.*)

SUSANNAH

Save the baby seals?

FRANK

That amongst other things. That as well. For all these kids you're going to have. The Greens aren't wrong. We are the custodians ... of the planet.

ACT TWO

SUSANNAH

Hah! (*She laughs.*) When were you any good at maintenance?

They both laugh.

FRANK

You'll need something.

SUSANNAH

Perhaps. I don't know. (*She ruffles his papers.*) So much ... paper.

FRANK

Recycled though.

She laughs.

FRANK

You must belong to something. I mean, you have to. Otherwise, it's just ...

She nods.

FRANK

Give us a try. There is a space. We can't pay much. You'd need something else as well. Think about it.

SUSANNAH

Perhaps.

FRANK

Have a look round, of course.

SUSANNAH

(*Pause*) Frank, I need a child. You could give me a child. You could give me a child here and now. If you like, I'll go away and never see you again. If you love her.

FRANK gets up and walks away. He plays with things on the table. Silence.

FRANK

It was fine at first. I was educated. A college boy. She thought she'd got a real bargain. She liked showing me off, doing her friends in the eye.

SUSANNAH

What about you?

FRANK

Oh, fantastic, just to be with her. It's a big aphrodisiac being with a woman other men want. And I'd done it ... married a straight-down-the-line working class girl. You'd have loved some of the confrontations with our more bourgeois friends.

She looks at him objectively.

FRANK

It wasn't the reason I'd married her, but it was damned exhilarating. We were both on a real high. And then the pregnancies. She was magnificent. Brave. Like a lion. God, bloody painful. (*He catches SUSANNAH's eye.*) She was fine. Eating steak and chips the minute Pete was out. (*Pause*) And then ... I don't know. She went back to work. We needed the bread. The hours are dodgy. It's a strain. You're on your feet all day. You're giving out to people. You've no idea what people tell their hairdressers. Christ, she's heard the lot! Little old ladies getting a last hairdo before a major cancer operation ... cheering up a woman who's just had her nose broken by her old man and wants something to make him fancy her on her birthday. The end of the day, we were

ACT TWO

both knackered, and with two young kids ... One's
all right. You can cope. But, with two it's a family.
They need ... (*He shrugs, pauses.*) And then ...
(*Slight pause.*) I don't know. I began to relax. Stopped
playing games. I let her get right in. She has that
contemptuous familiarity of people bred at close
quarters with no privacy – no respite for the mind.
She's used to quarrelling, picking fights. She gets
off on that. I can't do it. I couldn't rise, God, she can
be vicious! (*He walks about. Pause.*) She got bored.
Began to take me for granted. And there are all those
randy hairdressers. They're not all gay, believe me.
She'd tell me about it. Getting a quick one between
floors on the way down to the tinting. Parties. Pick-
ups. Musicians after a gig. Discos. Receptions. You
make big money doing hair privately. There'd be
dances, weddings. She'd get it from the waiters, the
best man, the bridegroom ... even the bloody bride!

SUSANNAH

She tells you?

FRANK

She's a blabbermouth. She doesn't like to feel uneasy.

SUSANNAH

Phew!

FRANK

She's settled down a bit. She has ... boyfriends.
There was a big Irishman, then an actor, then some
electronics wizard. This one – the one she's got now –
is really loaded. Formula One racing driver – man
about town. Knows the score. And tough. She likes a
man who's tough. I talk soft. I don't come on all the

time. I look for tenderness and she wants invention. What I ought to do is take a strap to her. She'd like that.

SUSANNAH

You're obsessed.

FRANK

Yes. She escapes me.

SUSANNAH

Oh, my dear.

He sits beside her, smiles and caresses her face.

SUSANNAH

You've been in my thoughts for years.

He makes to kiss her.

CRYSTAL appears in the doorway.

CRYSTAL

Ahhh!

She enters, genial, and puts down a bottle.

CRYSTAL

(*To SUSANNAH*) God, where the hell have you been? What's happened to your skin?

SUSANNAH

(*Standing awkwardly*) I've been working in Bolivia.

CRYSTAL

You didn't leave a day too soon.

SUSANNAH

You look wonderful.

ACT TWO

CRYSTAL

Drink?

SUSANNAH shakes her head.

CRYSTAL

Well, carry on. Don't mind me.

She sits, crossing her legs flamboyantly.

FRANK

Carry on what?

CRYSTAL jumps up with a clatter, making them both jump.

CRYSTAL

I know! Stereo! Wotcha fancy? (*Peering at SUSANNAH's face, en passant*) Christ! (*She fumbles with the records.*)

SUSANNAH

How are the children?

CRYSTAL

Oh, I expect he's been filling you in. With the details.

SUSANNAH

No, as a matter of fact, I've only just...

CRYSTAL

(*Puts on a disc. To FRANK:*) I thought you was goin' to the pictures?

FRANK

Changed my mind. So?

CRYSTAL

Well, it's a bit awkward.

FRANK

Why?

CRYSTAL

(*Moves about, restless*) Look ... Why don't we get sensible? I thought you was goin' to be out for a couple of hours. I got a friend coming in. I mean, I don't mind. You've kept it very dark ...

FRANK

What do you mean? There's nothing going on.

He looks to SUSANNAH for support, but she sits like a totem pole.

FRANK

Who's coming?

CRYSTAL

Nobody. Friend of mine.

FRANK

A girl?

CRYSTAL

No.

FRANK

Have you been making a habit of this?

CRYSTAL

Hark at him! You can tell 'e's a schoolmaster, can't you? That's how he goes on. Look, cock, this is my place.

FRANK

No, it isn't.

CRYSTAL

It bloody is.

SUSANNAH

(*Rising.*) I'd better go.

ACT TWO

FRANK

(*Irritable.*) No.

CRYSTAL

All I'm saying is: why don't we ...

FRANK

No!

CRYSTAL

(*A whine*) Frank ... He'll be here in a minute!

FRANK

I've told you – no!

CRYSTAL

Come on! You might as well.

FRANK

What? Might as well what?

CRYSTAL

(*Sullen*) It's not as though you don't know about it.
Look ...

FRANK

Shut up!!

There is a long silence. SUSANNAH makes to speak, but thinks better of it.

CRYSTAL

Right. That's it then. We know where we are.

SUSANNAH

Frank ...

CRYSTAL

All right for some.

FRANK

What are you talking about?

CRYSTAL

I'm not 'aving it.

FRANK

Having what?

CRYSTAL

You can make your mind up. What do you want to do? Do you want to finish?

He looks at her, aghast.

SUSANNAH

(*Seeing his face*) Crystal, I've only just come back. Frank and I haven't seen each other for ...

A LOUD KNOCK.

FRANK and CRYSTAL make for the door.

CRYSTAL

Shit!

FRANK

(*Pushing her out of the way*) Get out of it!

FRANK exits, followed by CRYSTAL.

SUSANNAH moves to the door, trying to see and hear.

SUSANNAH

Frank, don't!

FRANK

(*Offstage*) You, push off.

ACT TWO

HARRY

(*Offstage. Upper class voice*) What's the matter? What's going on?

CRYSTAL

(*Offstage*) Look love, it's off. Frank's got his girlfriend in.

HARRY

(*Offstage*) Has he now?

CRYSTAL

(*Offstage*) You better go.

HARRY

(*Offstage*) I'm coming in!

FRANK

(*Offstage*) Go on, get out! Out!

The SOUND OF A FIGHT.

SUSANNAH exits running.

SUSANNAH

(*Off*) Frank, don't!

CRYSTAL

(*Off*) Leave him alone, you bloody fool. Leave him alone! Get out of it, you big prick!

Sounds of a further scuffle.

SUSANNAH and CRYSTAL enter, supporting FRANK, who is now bleeding.

CRYSTAL exits. We hear her whispering urgently to HARRY.

CRYSTAL

(*Off*) Naow ... don't! No, you done enough already! How can I? ... I can't, can I?

HARRY

(*Off*) Listen, babe, make your fucking mind up.

CRYSTAL

(*Off*) Oh shove off!

CRYSTAL enters.

CRYSTAL

Now he's on the fucking turn.

SUSANNAH

(*Mopping FRANK's face*) Was he hurt?

CRYSTAL

You kiddin'?

CRYSTAL exits into the kitchen and quickly returns with a bowl of water, Band-aids, and Listerine.

CRYSTAL

Keep still.

CRYSTAL and SUSANNAH inspect the cut.

SUSANNAH

Is it deep?

CRYSTAL

I don't know. What do you think? Is it hurting, Frank?

He mumbles.

CRYSTAL

God, he's really out of it.

She puts on the antiseptic and a Bandaid.

FRANK

Ow!

ACT TWO

CRYSTAL

Sorry, love.

SUSANNAH lights up. She offers FRANK a cigarette. He shakes his head.

CRYSTAL exits with the bowl.

SUSANNAH

You all right?

CRYSTAL returns.

CRYSTAL

He'll be okay.

FRANK

(*To CRYSTAL*) So you were bringing him back here?

CRYSTAL

Yeah.

FRANK

Here, to our bed?

CRYSTAL

Yeah, why not?

FRANK

Sure, why not invite the kids in? Make a show.

CRYSTAL

There's no need to be filthy.

SUSANNAH

I think I'd better go.

FRANK

No, don't.

CRYSTAL
No, stay.

FRANK
It's not the first time, is it?

CRYSTAL
Forget it. You're upset.

SUSANNAH
I'd better go.

FRANK
No.

CRYSTAL
Sit down. Have a drink. I know, a cup of tea.

CRYSTAL exits.

FRANK follows her off. We hear their voices, prolonged.

SUSANNAH is uncertain whether to go or stay. The voices are raised. She picks up her bag to go. There is a screech from CRYSTAL.

She decides to stay.

Silence.

Now she is really non-plussed. What are they doing?

She goes to the kitchen door to listen. And just manages to step back as CRYSTAL enters regally with a tray of tea, a modern teapot, and a matching set of retro cups and saucers.

CRYSTAL
Sit down, Susannah. Make yourself at home. Like me cups? Present from Boy George. Sugar?

ACT TWO

SUSANNAH

Two please.

CRYSTAL

Bad for the skin.

SUSANNAH

Where's Frank?

CRYSTAL

He's lying down.

SUSANNAH

In the kitchen?

CRYSTAL

Mmm. Well? What d'you fink?

SUSANNAH

I beg your pardon?

CRYSTAL

Of him. Of me feller.

SUSANNAH

Sorry?

CRYSTAL

What did you think to 'im?

SUSANNAH

I didn't really get a good look.

CRYSTAL

Anyway, he's better with his clothes off. Ooh! That's better. (*She puts down her cup.*) You back for good?

SUSANNAH

Yes.

CRYSTAL

Not goin' abroad no more?

SUSANNAH

No.

CRYSTAL

Packed it in, eh?

SUSANNAH

Yes.

CRYSTAL

What you gonna do?

SUSANNAH

I haven't made my mind up.

CRYSTAL

There's not a lot about.

SUSANNAH

So I gather.

CRYSTAL

Still, you'll be able to pull something, eh? With your qualifications. Always room for your sort of work, eh?

SUSANNAH

Is he all right?

CRYSTAL

Sure. You don't look as if you've been 'avin' a good time.

SUSANNAH

You could say that.

ACT TWO

CRYSTAL

Make up for it! You're only young once. That's what my Mum says. Tell you what – come down to the salon. I'll give you a peel. A skin peel. For nothing. Cost you over fifty, you know. They vacuum your wallet soon as you come in the door. What about the Dance Studio? Be good for your neck, that.

SUSANNAH

What's wrong with my neck?

CRYSTAL

(*CRYSTAL manipulates SUSANNAH's neck.*) There! You see? Stiff! You're all rigid! There's a lot of stuff now. Dance. Exercise. Body-shaping. Look. (*She displays her body – does a flip and the splits.*) I used to be ever so thick here. And here. I do this every morning.

She demonstrates a floor exercise.

FRANK enters, and stands watching her. She sees him.

CRYSTAL

Frank, how are you feeling?

He doesn't reply. He finds an old grip behind the table and begins to throw things into it.

CRYSTAL

What do you think you're doing?

He glares at her, and continues to pack.

CRYSTAL

Don't be silly.

She tries to stop him.

FRANK

Get out. Leave it!

CRYSTAL

Frank...

FRANK

Will you get out of my way!

CRYSTAL

What are you looking for? There's nothing in that drawer. Frank! Look, don't be so stupid.

They scuffle.

SUSANNAH tries to intervene.

SUSANNAH

Please, stop it! Look, this is ridiculous.

SUSANNAH is hit on the nose.

SUSANNAH

Ow!

CRYSTAL

Now look what you've done! What do you think you're doing? (*She helps SUSANNAH to her feet.*) You shove Harry down the stairs. Just as well he was legless, he'd have given you a right pasting. Look at her nose! It'll be the size of a marrow in the morning. Susannah! (*She shouts as if SUSANNAH is unconscious.*) Susannah! You all right?

SUSANNAH

Oof... ooergh...

CRYSTAL

Oh Christ.

ACT TWO

CRYSTAL exits quickly and returns with a bowl, flannel, and the Listerine.

CRYSTAL

Fucking Florence Nightingale! I thought I was gonna 'ave a quiet night. (*She looks at FRANK.*) Crumbs – your eye!

FRANK

(*To SUSANNAH:*) I'm sorry. I didn't mean to hit you.

SUSANNAH

Ooh ...

CRYSTAL

Oh look. She looks terrible! Ah! Talk about Karl Malden. She hasn't set foot in this country five minutes. First thing you do ... Honest, I don't know. (*She ministers with quick confidence.*) Lie back.

SUSANNAH

I'm all right. No, really. I'm okay.

CRYSTAL

(*Inserting a tissue in one of SUSANNAH's nostrils.*) It'll be a week before she can see straight. Well, are you going or stopping?

FRANK glares at her. He sits abruptly, clutching his bag.

FRANK

(*To SUSANNAH*) I'm sorry, love.

SUSANNAH nods and tries to smile.

CRYSTAL

No thanks to you.

CRYSTAL exits into the kitchen with the bowl.

SUSANNAH

I should go.

FRANK

Where are you staying?

SUSANNAH

At the YW.

Enter CRYSTAL.

CRYSTAL

You're kidding. She can't stay there!

FRANK

Stay here. At least for the night. (*To CRYSTAL*) Okay?

CRYSTAL

Sure. Up to you.

FRANK

(*Sitting firmly.*) I'm going.

CRYSTAL

Leave it out.

FRANK

I'm going!

CRYSTAL

You're not. He's not, is he Susannah?

SUSANNAH

(*Speaking with difficulty, the tissue up her nose*)
Frank – you're upset. Why not sleep on it?

FRANK

Fouling her own nest. I'm not having that.

ACT TWO

CRYSTAL

Oh, don't be so ridiculous. Anyway, where do you think you're going? You can't go anywhere. You can't afford it for a start. Where's the bread coming from? You'd have to work!

FRANK

I do work.

CRYSTAL

Work?

FRANK

You try teaching kids...

CRYSTAL

I didn't mean that. I meant all your other stuff! (*Pause*) If it comes down to it, I'm the one to go. It's your place. Yours and hers. That's how it started. I'll go.

FRANK

Set you up, has he?

CRYSTAL

You kidding? If I get out of 'ere, I'm finding somefing decent for me and the kids.

FRANK

You're not taking the kids.

CRYSTAL

I'm not leavin' 'em.

SUSANNAH

Please. I'll go. Obviously, I'm the one to go. I can't bear to see him unhappy!

CRYSTAL

Him?! He never even got me a decent house. All the girls I was at school with have got good places. One's livin' in Wimbledon! I should 'ave gone in with Ray. I could've 'ad me own salon by now. But no, dirty word, innit, business. No cooperation at all. It's all right for me to work me arse off seven days a week. We-ell, I'm rubbish, aren't I? I'm getting veins now.

She displays an elegant leg.

FRANK

There's nothing wrong with your legs. You don't have to put in the hours. You do it because you want to.

CRYSTAL

(*To SUSANNAH*) You got any money?

SUSANNAH

Yes, I have, as a matter of fact. (*To FRANK*) Dad died.

FRANK

Oh, I'm sorry.

SUSANNAH

It was quick. Mark said he got up from the breakfast table, said: 'I think I'll just stroll over to the links,' and was dead before he hit the floor.

CRYSTAL stifles a giggle.

CRYSTAL

Leave a lot, did he?

SUSANNAH

Enough to buy a property.

CRYSTAL

Yeah? (*Slight pause*) Tell you what ...

ACT TWO

FRANK

Shut up.

CRYSTAL

I was only thinking.

Pause.

SUSANNAH

What? What were you thinking?

CRYSTAL

This girl I know. She's got a house. Some guy set her up. Actually, it's two houses knocked into one, so the garden's fantastic. You remember, Frank? I showed you.

He glares, and she pulls a resigned face.

CRYSTAL

It's a great house. She leaves dustbins and rubbish outside, you know, so's she don't get done over. But, inside, she's spent a fortune. It's all pale blue deco, with a studio out the back.

SUSANNAH

She wants to sell?

CRYSTAL

Yeah, she's marrying an Arab. I introduced them. (*Flicks a glance at FRANK.*) We could get it for nothing. Don't mean a thing to her and, like I say, she owes me a favour.

SUSANNAH

You mean I should buy it?

CRYSTAL

We could share. Frank, sit down.

SUSANNAH

Sit down, Frank. How do you mean, share, Crystal?

CRYSTAL

Well, the way I look at it ... I mean, if Frank and you think it's a good idea. (*To FRANK*) I mean, let's face it, love, it's okay in bed but I bore the tits off you when I open me mouth. I mean, sometimes I don't, but that's because I act up and make you laugh. Only you don't always feel like playing Betty Boop – know what I mean? (*To SUSANNAH*) Have you seen the kids?

SUSANNAH shakes her head.

CRYSTAL

Ah, you'll love them.

SUSANNAH gazes at her, mesmerized.

SUSANNAH

Will I?

CRYSTAL

They both look like Frank. (*Pause*) I've always felt bad about it. Taking him off you. I was potty for a baby. Frank happened to turn up at the right moment.

SUSANNAH

That looks painful. (*As FRANK favours his eye.*)

CRYSTAL

He'll be all right.

SUSANNAH wrings out a cloth in the bowl. He applies it to his eye.

SUSANNAH

(*To CRYSTAL*) You were saying?

ACT TWO

CRYSTAL

What?

SUSANNAH

About the house.

FRANK

Forget it.

He tries to rise. They press him back.

CRYSTAL

It's perfect for sharin.' There's lots of rooms. She's got them all done simple. The bedrooms are like little nun's cells. I mean, little cells for nuns, not little nuns ...

They giggle.

CRYSTAL

Then there's this huge, big kitchen. Two lounges, and another little room Frank could use as an office. It backs on to the cemetery ... (*Flicks a glance at FRANK*) ... so it's nice and quiet, for work.

FRANK looks at her without expression.

CRYSTAL

We've got some money, and we'll get something for the lease on this.

SUSANNAH

Frank?

FRANK

No.

SUSANNAH

Frank ...

FRANK

Susannah!

She retires, defeated. Slight pause.

CRYSTAL

It could work, love.

FRANK

Fuck off.

CRYSTAL

Oh, come on! What's all the sulking for? You know I've always had a bit on the side. Don't be so double-faced. What's the matter? Are you afraid of bein' shown up in front of Susannah? Look, I'm not like you two. I don't want to get it out of books. I like living!

They look at her without response.

CRYSTAL

I just think it could work, that's all. The three of us.

FRANK looks from one girl to the other without response.

CRYSTAL

Look at him. He wants the best of both! What a face! No good-looking like you want to wring my neck. You done me out of a bit of hey diddle-diddle, mate. You know what your trouble is? You think too much. Look, tell you what. Why don't you have a talk about it? I'll push off. Go to bed. You two have a talk. Sort it out ... okay?

FRANK

(*Low and furious*) And you've got all the answers. What do you mean, sort it out? What's that supposed to mean? We're married. We have two children. You

ACT TWO

know what my plans are. You agreed! You agreed
about me chucking the teaching.

CRYSTAL

Sure. Fine.

FRANK

I'm doing it off your back, and I know very well
you've no idea – not the faintest idea – what I'm about,
any more than you ever have. I'm not blaming you.
Simply stating a fact. I take full responsibility for
the marriage, for ... Just the same. Just the same ...
(*He puts his head in his hands momentarily.*) It *is*
a marriage. We have created a marriage. We are
a family. There are your parents, my parents. (*To
SUSANNAH*) I know *you'll* understand. There are
facts and truths and values here. I'm not prepared to
overturn, not just *my* life. God knows, that's worth
little enough – not a swallow would be affected. Oh,
I'm well aware of that ... of what the world thinks.
My mates. (*To CRYSTAL*) You. Nonetheless ...
Nonetheless, it is our marriage.

He looks up at CRYSTAL without expression.

CRYSTAL

I know you've put a lot in. You don't want to waste
it. Nobody wants to think they've wasted their life.
But I'm not a fucking ornament. And I don't need you
trying to tell me what to do. Why don't you work your
own patch for a change? For Christ's sakes, can't you
see? She's bloody grieving for you!

SUSANNAH

Crystal, please.

CRYSTAL

Right. Nothing to do with me, right? Only I'm not having my kids messed about. There'll be no splittin' off out of it. Might do for some, not for me. We got a solution. (*To FRANK*) If you can just get your fuckin' jealousy out of it.

Pause

FRANK

(*Low*) I'll kill you. And myself. And the kids.

Silence.

CRYSTAL

(*Mutters*) It's what it's all about. What it's always been about. Watch it, Susannah. They're not going to change.

Silence.

FRANK

I ... I don't know what to do any more. I try. But I don't seem to be able to ... The women yell and complain, and I see it. I accept the argument. And I wash the nappies, and the kid's clothes. And I wait at the school gate. And you don't respect me. If I were a bugger you'd respect me. But because I try to respect you, you don't.

CRYSTAL

I'm not yours. You don't own me. (*Pause*) If you want me to go, I'll go. But the kids come with me.

He gives her a dangerous look.

ACT TWO

SUSANNAH

No. I'll go. This is all my fault. I should never have ... (*She falters and begins to cry.*) It's just that I ... I want ... (*She cries.*)

CRYSTAL

(*Full of sympathy*) Ah!

SUSANNAH

I'm sorry.

CRYSTAL

No, go on. Have a good cry. (*She cuddles SUSANNAH.*) It's him, isn't it?

SUSANNAH

Does it show?

CRYSTAL

When you're with him. Always did. I done you out of it. I'm the one to go.

SUSANNAH

No.

FRANK

I'm bloody going.

CRYSTAL

We can't all go.

Pause.

CRYSTAL

Stay then.

Pause.

SUSANNAH

Frank?

CRYSTAL

Frank? Ah, look at his poor eye. Shall I see if Inez has got a steak?

FRANK

Stuff it.

He rises and looms over her dangerously.

Then he exits into the bedroom.

SUSANNAH

How big is the garden?

CRYSTAL

A hundred feet, and round the side.

SUSANNAH

Wow!

CRYSTAL

And there's a conker tree.

FRANK returns. He is stuffing clothes into his bag.

CRYSTAL

I said I'd let her know.

SUSANNAH

Frank?

He looks from one to the other. And slams out.

SUSANNAH

Damn.

CRYSTAL

Don't worry.

SUSANNAH

His poor eye.

ACT TWO

CRYSTAL

He'll be all right.

SUSANNAH

Do you think he ... I mean, has he ... ?

CRYSTAL

Nah. Don't think so. Do you?

SUSANNAH

I don't know. He does have a tendency to pop his cork.

CRYSTAL

He'll be back.

SUSANNAH

I wonder.

CRYSTAL

He's left his books.

SUSANNAH

(*Doubtful*) Mmm.

CRYSTAL

Oh well. Soon find out. More tea. Oh, it's cold. I know, drop of the ruin. Be good for your nose.

SUSANNAH

I doubt it but thanks. Yes, I will.

CRYSTAL

Put your feet up.

She crosses to the record player, puts on '*How Long Blues*' by Jimmy Yancy.

SUSANNAH

D'you think he ... ?

CRYSTAL

Relax. Don't worry about it.

She gives SUSANNAH a drink. She picks up her own drink, in a long glass. She sashays to the music, glass in hand.

SUSANNAH drinks, lies back and relaxes. She looks around the room she has thought of so often, taking it all in again. She feels comfortable and warm, and where she wants to be.

She sighs aloud. A long sigh.

CRYSTAL

What?

SUSANNAH

I mean ... is it too much to ask?

CRYSTAL

What?

SUSANNAH

You seem to manage.

CRYSTAL

(*With an eloquent gesture towards the door.*) You joking?

SUSANNAH

(*Giggles*) He always was an old chauve. Well, they all are.

CRYSTAL

Yeah, and rapists.

SUSANNAH

(*Getting a bit drunk.*) Oh no, not Frank! No.

CRYSTAL

(*Ruefully*) No.

SUSANNAH laughs.

ACT TWO

CRYSTAL

What's he been telling you?

SUSANNAH

Nothing.

CRYSTAL

No, go on. (*She makes to sit by SUSANNAH, but jumps up.*) I'll bring the bottle.

SUSANNAH

Listen, was that the door?

CRYSTAL

(*Shakes her head*) He'll be down the pub, drowning his miseries. Look, forget it. Let him do what he wants.

SUSANNAH

But we need to talk this over.

CRYSTAL

Sod him. Who needs him? Here, what's he been tellin' you?

She adds gin to SUSANNAH's glass.

SUSANNAH

Nothing really. Well ...

SUSANNAH laughs and tilts slightly.

Then she and CRYSTAL, heads together, begin to gossip and giggle. Their voices are inaudible under the MUSIC of the blues.

Fade to black.

The End

AFTERWORD

LEFTIES IN LOVE

Three into two won't go. An old theme perhaps, but in Pam Gems' new play, LOVING WOMEN, there's a twist.

Susannah loves Frank, but Frank has fallen for Crystal, leaving heartache and bitterness in his wake. A triangular relationship, but with one crucial difference. These characters are from the revolutionary left. They are the new guard, but trapped in the same grooves, trodden by countless past generations. LOVING WOMEN is not an idealistic play.

Feelings of outrage prompted Pam Gems to write it after she had read a biography of J Middleton Murray (crony of D H Lawrence), written by his son. The book described Murray's first two marriages, one to writer Katherine Mansfield, and one to someone just like her. Both women died of TB, and he then took his nurse Betty as a bride.

Betty was, as Pam describes, 'everything they were not. Working class, healthy, robust, noisy and unintellectual.' LOVING WOMEN is in her memory.

The play, half set in 1973, half in the present, is a timely criticism of the left's patronising attitude to working class women. It's honest about sexual attraction too.

Crystal is a hairdresser. She dresses up, wears make-up, reveals her cleavage, likes money, dislikes polemic. Susannah is a social worker, earnest and dedicated. Frank is caught between the two – a good lefty, but desperately drawn to Crystal's Monroe wiggle. Sexual preference does not change with the revelations of Marx. And a working-class family does not mean that Crystal is not as bright as the other two put together.

Pam Gems' poor background makes her naturally

antagonistic towards pretension from any 'radical' quarter – whether social work socialism (hence Frank's statement, 'It's us and valium instead of a decent housing policy') or middle-class feminism.

She remembers the early Miss World protests, and says: 'If I was 18 and could make £2000 out of beauty contest, and get out of a factory job, then nothing would stop me.'

Class is an important issue for Pam Gems, and she has turned to a working-class director, Phil Davis, for a trustworthy interpretation of her work. She adds, 'I also didn't want it to be a feminist hatchet job on men.'

Wary of feminists perhaps, but Pam Gems makes some harsh judgements on men herself. Her views verge on biological determinism, as she is calmly convinced that men in their personalities and behaviour 'are more regressive than women.' The key lies with the XY chromosome. XX (female) is a much more sturdy formula, she feels.

In the play, Frank is certainly more vulnerable than either Crystal or Susannah. He suffers crippling self-doubt – and despite his residual affection for Susannah, and his failed marriage to Crystal, it is he who refuses the proposal of a shared open house with the two women. Some empty memory of the 'sanctity of marriage' represses even such a revolutionary stalwart as himself.

But Frank is not a scapegoat. The strength of this play is that there are no heroes and heroines. Each character has insights to offer as well as weaknesses to hide.

BARNEY BARDSLEY. *City Limits*. 09/02/1984

NATALYA

In Memory of Assia Wevill

FOREWORD

In the 1930s, there was a tendency among the English intelligentsia towards Marxism. The First World War had left terrible scars, and the despotic aspects of British imperialism sickened a generation exposed to four years of military idiocy.

Marxism was idealistic, and so it was fashionable to be pro-Russian, despite published information as to the fearsome and repressive nature of the Soviet regime. World War II and Hitler's eastern invasion made bedfellows of Russia and the West, to be followed immediately by a stand-off between the two emergent world powers, and the Cold War.

But idealism is not easily snuffed out. In the new prosperity of the 60s and 70s, neo-Marxism flourished. To be on the left was de rigueur. Every political grouping claimed to be lefter than thou (good old English puritanism conjoining by chance with the gentle forbearances of the hippy movement.)

Television directors sat on expensive black sofas proclaiming power to the people. A famous actress stood outside the Soho Poly Theatre in the rain handing out leaflets, an old scarf tied round her head like a Holocaust victim – gesture politics from a woman who had never been without a hot bath in her life.

It was, in a way, endearing, even heart-warming, to see a new generation so well-fed and unoppressed that they could play mock politics – viz the 1968 Paris "uprising" when the Comedie Francaise got trashed.

In the 1980s, Margaret Thatcher said: "There is no such thing as society." Consumerism was God. Well, who doesn't want a warm, dry house and toys? And then the Berlin wall came down and the invasion of the West by the rest of the world began.

How to stop it? Perhaps political refugees could be accepted, but the poor as well? Could these invasions be legitimated? Mea culpa had been a liberal theme since the turn of the century.

It is not fashionable now to write overtly political plays. In the 70s it was mandatory. Those of us who chose to hide the emetic under the jam, and attempted restraint from imposition, were likely to be dismissed as marginal, if not reactionary.

Dramatic metaphor today is polarised between the cute and the impenetrable. You pick your shtick – not, you hope, as laughably non-existent as the Emperor's new clothes, neither inaccessibly Manichean – that condescending mode – nor irrelevantly exciting. Writers have many weapons: suspense, terror, titillation and humour (the most lethal and the least respected.)

For a play about today I summoned the memory of a woman I once knew. She was a Russian Jewess who, having escaped from Nazi Germany, had married a man she loathed in order to get British citizenship. She was stunningly and exotically beautiful, cultured, multi-lingual, highly intelligent, and cut a swathe through the 50s-literary world. She had a penchant for poets.

But, underneath, there was detachment. She suffered from depressions. And there was always the underlying contempt: "What do you know?"

As a species, we are troubled by injustice, thank God. In the prosperous, industrialised West there is still want and deprivation for so many people. Why? We have the information, the solutions – enough to feed and house the world. Perhaps all we need is love, or at least instruction on how and why to respect the needs of strangers.

In St. Petersburg recently, a tired and respectable-looking

man offered me a currency deal on the street. I said I was leaving for London the next day and offered him cigarettes for goodwill. He went red with humiliation, and walked away.

The real-life model for Natalya is dead. In NATALYA, the play, she is a survivor. Criminal of course.

Pam Gems
2001

NATALYA

CAST

CAROLLE	late twenties.
EBBA	about thirty, attractive.
MICHELENE	mid-thirties.
ROGER	mid-thirties, gay.
JACK	around forty.
BRIAN	mid-thirties
NATALYA	late twenties, beautiful.
BA	twenty-six, Downs Syndrome.

NATALYA

ACT ONE

ACT ONE – SCENE ONE

A London loft-style interior with a view of the river.

A big sofa with pale grey loose covers and cushions, a low table, other seating and a desk, on which sits the latest Apple desk-top computer.

At the desk is an orthopaedic chair, the sort you kneel forward on. In a corner a stuffed moose acts as a clothes hanger and hat and scarf rack.

It's a sunny day.

The DOORBELL rings. Pause. Another ring. Pause.

CAROLLE enters. She is big and ungainly, with depressing hair, wears a jacket, a longish skirt and flat shoes. She has a punishingly heavy shoulder bag which pulls her down on one side. She looks around the room.

CAROLLE

Hullo!

She waits but there is no reply, so she has a snoop.

She hears a sound, jumps away from the desk and moves swiftly to the sofa and sits, her bag on her lap.

EBBA enters. She is comely, late twenties, maybe thirty, with a lot of hair, attractively styled. She is wearing a bath towel.

CAROLLE makes to rise but EBBA, not seeing her, crosses to the computer and starts to work.

CAROLLE rises, sits and fidgets, fearing to interrupt.

EBBA finishes, prints out, picks up paper, sees CAROLLE.

EBBA

Oh, hi. Won't be a moment.

She goes.

CAROLLE rises as the front door slams.

MICHELENE enters. She is fashionably thin, with a short trendy haircut, wears high heels and an immaculate pale green suit. She is carrying a similar suit, in pink, on a hanger.

MICHELENE

(Calls) Ebba! *(She looks at her watch, and sees CAROLLE.)*

CAROLLE

She just – she was – she's ...

MICHELENE

Right. *(Assesses CAROLLE dismissively.)* D'you mind? I need this room. There'll be a celebrity here any moment to interview Miss Marriner.

CAROLLE

Yes. Sorry.

MICHELENE

So, if you could ...

She puts out an arm, to usher CAROLLE out.

CAROLLE

It's me.

ACT ONE

MICHELENE

What?

CAROLLE

There was a mix-up over dates, and we go to press, so I'm doing it. Carolle Carpenter. *(She puts out a hand which MICHELENE ignores.)*

EBBA wanders in, now in loose trousers and a silk top with pushed-up sleeves.

MICHELENE

(To EBBA) Do you know about this?

EBBA

I'm sorry?

MICHELENE

We're pulling out. *(To CAROLLE)* Sorry about this.

CAROLLE

But the photographer's on his way!

MICHELENE

Tough.

CAROLLE

It's Roger Moth!

MICHELENE

Roger Moth? *(Placated, to EBBA)* Photographer of the year. Showed at the Biennale. Where is he?

CAROLLE fishes in her bag for her mobile, talks in the background.

CAROLLE

Roger? Where are you? Crumbs, no! Not Place – Gardens. Can you see the river? Oh, you're in the pub. Turn left outside … No, left or you'll fall in. First right – two minutes ... No, now – Roger please – yes, waiting. Look, Roger ... *(But he has gone.)*

While she is telephoning, MICHELENE displays the suit to EBBA.

EBBA

New?

MICHELENE

Your outfit. For the shoot.

EBBA

Michelene! You want me to look like Joan Collins?

MICHELENE

Who may not be Sarah Bernhardt but is *always* well-groomed.

She thrusts the suit at EBBA, fishes in her bag, and takes out huge, slightly tinted glasses. She shoves them on EBBA's nose.

EBBA

I can't look like this.

MICHELENE

Why not?

EBBA

Because I'm not mental. What have you done with my brother?

MICHELENE

Brian's at the lab.

EBBA

Does he know you don't want children?

The DOORBELL rings, loud and insistent.

EBBA goes, followed by MICHELENE with the suit.

ACT ONE

VOICES offstage.

MICHELENE

(Offstage) In there.

ROGER erupts into the room. He is late-thirties, charismatic, gay.

ROGER

(Sees CAROLLE) Ah, Laughing Girl. What have we got?

CAROLLE

Lady novelist.

ROGER

Oh, dog!

CAROLLE

(Hisses) Roger!

MICHELENE strides in with a drinks tray.

MICHELENE

Roger Moth? I adore your work. I'm Michelene Whelan. *(To CAROLLE)* soon to be Marriner actually. I'm marrying Ebba's brother Brian Marriner, the scientist. Now, how shall we do this?

ROGER

Vodka tonic please.

MICHELENE

(Pouring.) We're terribly protective with our novelists. *(To CAROLLE:)* Half an hour?

CAROLLE

I was hoping for in-depth.

MICHELENE waves the vodka bottle at her.

CAROLLE

Sorry, could I have tea?

EBBA enters, having tidied her hair and pulled down her sleeves as a concession to the interview.

EBBA

Of course. *(To MICHELENE)* I'd love a cup.

MICHELENE glares at her, and turns to CAROLLE.

MICHELENE

Indian? China?

CAROLLE

Er ... do you have Celestial?

MICHELENE

Possibly. *(At the door)* There's Gunpowder.

She goes.

ROGER leaps about, setting up. He gives EBBA the once-over and an approving nod.

EBBA

Michelene's a great publicist.

CAROLLE looks at her.

EBBA

She's a little wired at the moment. She's getting married.

CAROLLE

To your brother.

EBBA

Yes.

ACT ONE

CAROLLE

She said. How did they meet?

EBBA

(Glumly) Through me.

EBBA turns her head this way and that as ROGER takes Polaroids, and peers at them.

CAROLLE

Big wedding?

EBBA

Eight bridesmaids.

ROGER

Whoo-whoo!

CAROLLE

I didn't think people still did that. I mean, real people.

EBBA

I know what you mean.

CAROLLE

Not that I've got anything against
marriage – families ...

EBBA

Oh, she doesn't want children.

CAROLLE is shocked.

CAROLLE

Why not?

Flustered, CAROLLE delves into her bag, takes out two tape recorders.

CAROLLE

Could you ... ?

EBBA

(Into the recorder) Once more unto the breach dear friends, once more.

CAROLLE plays it back. Nothing comes out.

CAROLLE

I've got some batteries somewhere.

EBBA

Use the other one.

CAROLLE

That's the stand-by.

MICHELENE enters with tea, and a big CHOCOLATE CAKE. She sets it down, and cuts slices.

MICHELENE

Let's be wicked.

ROGER takes a large piece.

ROGER

(Mouth full.) Mmmmm!

EBBA

(Mildly.) I was keeping the cake for Ba.

MICHELENE ignores this, and bends over CAROLLE.

MICHELENE

You look hypoglycemic. Who's your homeopath?

CAROLLE

Fotini. Well she was. *(She eats cake, looks up.)* Until she started getting terse with me – I don't know why.

ROGER

(To EBBA) Just act naturally. *(Crouching)* Ignore me. *(He shoots up her crotch.)*

ACT ONE

MICHELENE

Who are you with now?

CAROLLE

Hans.

MICHELENE

Hans the Hunk, from Hungary?

CAROLLE

He says I've got sad shoulders. I'm on hypericum. For stress.

MICHELENE

Tell me about it.

MICHELINE crashes her cup back in its saucer, and rises.

MICHELENE

Right. I'll leave you to it.

She pushes the vodka bottle towards ROGER, then goes, balancing the tray.

CAROLLE fiddles with the batteries.

CAROLLE

(*Into the tape*) I've swopped over.

She plays back the tape.

TAPE

I've swopped over.

EBBA

Good. We'll start, shall we?

CAROLLE

Yes. Notebook ... notebook, in case the tape ... My specs!

EBBA takes them from the top of CAROLLE's head, and gives them to her. ROGER crashes about.

CAROLLE arranges herself, and starts the interview.

> CAROLLE

When did you start to write?

> EBBA

At school.

> CAROLLE

(Refers to her file.) St Godolphin's, right?

> EBBA

Yes.

> CAROLLE

(Brightening) You're Catholic?

> EBBA

No. Why, are you?

> CAROLLE

I'm a convert.

> EBBA

(Interested) Really? Why did you . . . ?

> CAROLLE

I'm not sure. I was lonely, I think. I have found the virgin birth rather hard to swallow. They say it has happened though.

> EBBA

It would certainly make life simpler.

EBBA squeaks as ROGER suddenly looms up beside her.

CAROLLE stands back and watches as ROGER takes over, snapping, and leaping about theatrically. She sighs.

ACT ONE

EBBA looks at her in enquiry. She shrugs.

> CAROLLE
>
> I was just thinking that I'll never be famous enough for Roger to do me.

ROGER pulls a face at EBBA behind CAROLLE'S back.

> EBBA
>
> Why not?

ROGER crashes about.

> CAROLLE
>
> I do write.

> EBBA
>
> Yes? What sort of thing do you ... ?

> CAROLLE
>
> Short stories. Well, a couple.

> EBBA
>
> Great.

> CAROLLE
>
> I expect you find it useful living with Jack Hansen.

> EBBA
>
> I'm not with him.

> CAROLLE
>
> Oh?

She grabs her notebook, leans forward, eyes gleaming at a possible scoop.

> EBBA
>
> I mean, I'm not published by his company.

CAROLLE

Oh. Still...

EBBA

We try not to talk shop.

CAROLLE

What do you talk about?

EBBA

The size of his cock, usually.

ROGER falls over.

EBBA

Sorry. That was a joke.

CAROLLE

How long have you been together?

EBBA

Three years.

CAROLLE

Not married.

EBBA

No.

CAROLLE

He's not prepared to commit?

EBBA

I'm sorry?

JACK enters.

JACK

Hullo.

ACT ONE

EBBA

Ask him.

JACK

Hullo, Babes. *(Bends, and kisses EBBA.)* Got a surprise for you!

EBBA

What?

JACK

Da-da!

NATALYA enters. She is very beautiful.

JACK

Meet Natalya.

ROGER, knocked out, begins to take pictures.

NATALYA

Hullo.

EBBA

(Rises) Hullo ...

CAROLLE

(Dazzled) Sorry – who?

NATALYA

Natalya Ivanovna. *(Taking JACK's arm.)* I am Mrs Jack Hansen.

Blackout.

ACT ONE - SCENE TWO

The Living Room. Later.

EBBA and JACK are sitting. NATALYA is sprawled comfortably on the sofa.

She rises.

> NATALYA
>
> I must make water.

NATALYA goes out.

> EBBA
>
> Jesus.

> JACK
>
> What can I say? She was in trouble.

> EBBA
>
> So, you married her?

> JACK
>
> To get her out. That was the deal.

> EBBA
>
> Deal? A deal is two-way, Jack. What do you get out of it?

> JACK
>
> Feelings of nobility?

> EBBA
>
> Oh, so you've kept your hands off her?

> JACK
>
> Well, actually – no.

Silence.

ACT ONE

EBBA

Auden didn't find it necessary to sleep with Erika Mann when he married her to get her out of Germany.

JACK

Yes, but we had to make it look good. There was this blessing in church, after the civil ceremony in Moscow. God, you should have seen it, Eb! Dark blue cupola against a pale blue sky. Pine trees. Young priest with a black beard. Incense. Then, at her friends' house, they put us in this bedroom.

EBBA

And you jumped her.

JACK

Other way round. She said it was only fair.

EBBA

(Sarcastic) Oh well, in that case ...

JACK

Her background's amazing. White Russian. One of her grandfathers is descended from Catherine the Great.

EBBA

Not the Small?

NATALYA enters. She takes JACK aside, and talks to him quietly.

EBBA

What is it? What are you talking about?

JACK

She wants our room.

EBBA

What?

NATALYA murmurs to him in urgent Russian.

JACK

(*Apologetic*) It's the birch tree, outside the window. She says it reminds her of ...

EBBA

Oh, for God's sake, take it.

NATALYA

Thank you. Now I am home. Here. (*Touches her chest.*) You have hair-dryer?

EBBA

In the bathroom.

NATALYA

(*Lifts her hair.*) My hair is full of Russia.

NATALYA Goes.

EBBA

Got my man. Got my room. If she gets pregnant, I'll kill you both.

JACK

Oh, there's no chance of that!

EBBA

Sure, are you?

JACK

Yes.

EBBA

Are you?

She flicks him across the face with a scarf, making him wince. She does it again.

ACT ONE

JACK

Cut it out!

EBBA

Cut it out? Cut it out? I'll cut it off!

She makes to go for him again. He grabs her wrist. A tussle. He pins her down.

JACK

We'll see.

Enter CAROLLE

CAROLLE

(*At the door*) Sorry. My car's been towed.

JACK climbs off EBBA, and exits with CAROLLE.

EBBA prowls the stage, furious. She turns on the radio.

It is *Shostakovich*, very loud.

JACK comes back.

She throws a vase at him. He ducks, and then rugby tackles her to the floor.

They wrestle violently, grunting and gasping.

Fade to black.

ACT ONE – SCENE THREE

The Living Room. Six weeks later.

JACK and EBBA cuddle together on the sofa. EBBA leans down, looking at her book on the floor.

JACK

Where's Natalya?

EBBA

Dunno. Gone to Tonga, I hope. Listen. *(Reads)* 'The caterpillar of the silver-wash fritillary needs beds of violet to feed on. Not so the butterfly itself. For that, bramble and thistle flowers must be provided.'

JACK

So?

EBBA

First course violets, then brambles and thistle.

JACK

(Kisses her.) What are you on about?

EBBA

I'll get fat. My books will go out of fashion.

JACK

No, they won't.

EBBA

I'll get fat.

JACK

I heard you.

EBBA

Still. *(Leans up on her elbow.)* There must be some compensations. Mustn't there?

JACK doesn't answer.

EBBA

I suppose ... I suppose having children renews you. *(Slight change of atmosphere.)* Replication. The

ACT ONE

rebirth of a self. Other, but connected. *(No response)* I do feel curious. *(No response.)* But not you.

JACK

Don't need no-one else. Just you.

EBBA

My publicist – and sister-in-law to be – doesn't want kids either. I am never to be an aunt, it seems. *(A thought stops her.)* Why my brother? Why Brian?

JACK

Because he's there?

EBBA

She did hit the ground running when there was that rumour of a Nobel prize.

JACK

Why's he doing it?

EBBA

He feels sorry for her.

JACK

(Sits up.) Sorry for her? For Michelene Whelan?

EBBA

I think so, yes.

JACK

Why?!

EBBA

Because she's unlikable.

Enter NATALYA, looking sensational, and carrying bags.

NATALYA

Potatoes!

JACK

Hi, Natale.

EBBA

Potatoes?

NATALYA

For Russian soup. Good for consolation.

EBBA

I don't need consolation. Why do I need consolation?

NATALYA

Is for me.

EBBA

You failed your test. (*To JACK*) Jack – vodka.

JACK goes.

NATALYA

The man is stupid. Not even impact! You know why he fails me? His teeth fall out.

EBBA

Natalya. Don't drive. Don't even dream of being a motorist. Wipe it from the blackboard of your imagination. True, my life would resume its normal course if you left us in a box, but think of the cremation arrangements. The immigration hassles when we want to ship out your ashes.

NATALYA

I must drive.

EBBA

Why?

ACT ONE

NATALYA

Because I cannot afford taxis every day!

EBBA

Use public transport!

NATALYA

Not possible.

EBBA

Why not? The rest of us manage it.

NATALYA

I am molested.

EBBA looks at her, and concedes the likelihood of this.

NATALYA

In any case, he gives me car.

EBBA

Your film producer?

NATALYA

Nah, nah. Porsche is from Gray-ham. You don't know him.

EBBA

A Porsche?! *(Whistles.)* Who's Graham?!

NATALYA

Sweet man. Very little but so generous. Ach, I leave him in Liberty House! I am asking to him to hold tape measure, then I think – oh, my present for Ebba ... I am close to Kaspia ... Nice shop ...

EBBA

Hadn't you better go and get him?

NATALYA

De nada.

EBBA

He might want his Porsche back.

NATALYA

Too late, I already sold it. (*Unwrapping a huge tin of caviare.*) For you!

EBBA

Natalya! Caviare? This must have cost a fortune!

NATALYA

(*Calls.*) Jack ... vodka! (*To EBBA*) You don't mind I sleep with Jack?

EBBA

Well ...

NATALYA

I like so much the English gentleman ...

EBBA

Hah!

NATALYA

Without class system, what is left? Money? Not romantic. Duchess – Your Majesty ... welcome to castle, Serene Highness.

EBBA

It's crap and you know it.

NATALYA

Ah, Jack ...

JACK enters with bottle and glasses.

ACT ONE

JACK

Vodka!

NATALYA

(Dives into a bag and produces, with a flourish)
Blinis ... crème fraiche ... plates!

EBBA

Oh, these are beautiful! Where did you ... ?

NATALYA

Thomas Goode. Nice shop.

EBBA

(Admiring plates) From Graham? The film producer?

NATALYA

I borrow.

EBBA winces.

NATALYA

The film producer ... verflucht.

They sit on the floor and eat from the tin.

NATALYA

He wants me for film. Original script. Woman who hates herself. I say, in Russia we know all this, and much more. It is banal, your script.

EBBA

And?

NATALYA

(Mouth full.) They like you to agree with them, film producers.

JACK

This is great.

NATALYA

Beluga. The best. Don't need lemon juice ... egg, onion – only when caviare is bad.

JACK

Slancheh! (*Irish pronunciation of Slainte: 'Good health!*)

They drink.

JACK

Yow!

EBBA

My God, Natalya! Do you always knock it back like that? Your liver!

NATALYA

Nah, nah, nah. All bad liver in Russia extinct centuries ago. Only warriors survive!

They knock back the caviare, and drink some more.

NATALYA

(*Lying back.*) Oh, I feel so good. Maybe I volunteer for good works. You think I am the type, Jack?

JACK

No.

NATALYA

(*To EBBA.*) You see? (*Sighs*) I tried before, but I was refused.

EBBA

Why?

NATALYA

Wrong shoes.

ACT ONE

EBBA

(*To JACK*) Did she tell you? A guy gave her a car and she sold it.

JACK

How much?

NATALYA

Ten thousand.

JACK

What are you going to do with the dough?

NATALYA

It is sent already to Russia. To my brother.

JACK

He's in trouble?

NATALYA

Nah, nah. (*She staggers to her feet.*) I must go to clinic.

EBBA

(*Alarmed*) Why, what's wrong?

NATALYA

To sell blood. I am rare type ... one hundred pounds each time.

EBBA

(*She is getting drunk*) Fuck, I'm only bloody boring A. (*of JACK*) He's even more boring ...

NATALYA

He can sell his come. Intelligent, tall, handsome Caucasian ... good sperm fetch good price.

EBBA

Imagine ... lots of little Jacks ...

NATALYA

Very nice.

EBBA

He doesn't think so. You watch – he'll get up and leave the room.

JACK

It's that or fuck you both.

NATALYA

Later, when I am bloodless. He can be Dracula.

She picks up Ebba's coat, puts it on her shoulders, and goes.

EBBA

That's my only good coat.

Pause.

JACK

There's something ... Bovary about her ... don't you think? Come on – you find her intriguing.

EBBA

A bloody great pain in the ass, you mean. I'm not enjoying the complicity between you, so don't be misled because I pretend I do.

JACK

A ship that passes in the night!

EBBA

Oh, that's a good phrase. Wish I'd thought of that.

ACT ONE

JACK

You will, Oscar. *(Lies back.)* I'm sitting on Brighton Pier ... thinking about you, of course ... breathing in the good sea air ... look out to sea – a boat ... long way off.

EBBA

What sort of a boat?

JACK

Don't know, too far away. Sleek ... comely. I watch it for a bit then a seagull yeeks and I throw it my cheese sandwich, and when I look up the boat is gone. That's it. C'est tout. A faint memory trace.

They embrace. She puts a leg over him.

EBBA

Is this me or her?

JACK

You. She's all warty and freckly.

EBBA

There isn't a wart on her.

JACK

She's a hooligan.

EBBA

You like hooligans.

She jumps on him.

Blackout.

ACT ONE – SCENE FOUR

The Living Room.

NATALYA, feet up on the sofa, is reading.

EBBA enters, laden with shopping. She begins to disgorge. Toilet rolls fall out. She picks one up.

NATALYA

Disgusting.

EBBA

(Holding it up) Why?

NATALYA

This colour, that colour – ach!

EBBA

Whole forests felled for bourgeois butts ...

NATALYA

So boring, all these choices. When can you think?

EBBA

Think? *(Flops down, lies back.)* Who thinks? Do you think? I don't. Thoughts ... arrive, but that's different.

NATALYA

Because you are lazy and corrupt. You don't think of the depth ... of what is for. Only the frivolous.

EBBA

So, what do you think about? Back in old Petersburg.

ACT ONE

NATALYA

Survival. Bargain for parachute silk from air force colonel to make knickers. Exchange for mascara. Queue for oranges. Time for thought then, believe me.

EBBA

Oranges?

NATALYA

And when it is your turn, they are green, and with withers.

EBBA

Withered. Shrivelled. Withers means something else.

NATALYA

What else?

EBBA

Part of a horse ... here ...

She touches NATALYA on the neck. NATALYA kisses her on the mouth.

EBBA

What did you do that for?

NATALYA

I thought you wanted. Are you not in love with me?

EBBA

(*Squeaky voice*) Of course not. Why – did you think I was gay? Homosexual?

NATALYA

Homosexual, heterosexual, what is the difference?

EBBA

You mean you'll sleep with anybody?

NATALYA
(Makes a hole with finger and thumb, puts in her index finger.) Not important.

EBBA
Who's corrupt now? All this pure talk about thinking!

NATALYA
I think so much better on back.

She smiles up at EBBA who laughs.

EBBA
You're having me on.

NATALYA
Have you where? I don't understand.

EBBA
It's a phrase. It means, you're teasing me.

NATALYA
You never sell the body?

EBBA
Of course not.

NATALYA
Not from obligation? To pay debt – for nice meal?

EBBA
No!

NATALYA
Not even as apology . . . ?

EBBA
No!!

ACT ONE

NATALYA

Oh well. *(She looks EBBA up and down.)* Maybe not.

The DOORBELL rings.

EBBA looks at NATALYA who shrugs.

EBBA exits to door.

NATALYA picks up a book, puts her feet up on the sofa, out of sight of the others.

EBBA enters, followed by MICHELENE.

MICHELENE

Look, I'm sorry. I'll have her some other time.

EBBA

I've told you, it's all right.

MICHELENE

Anyway, Ba much prefers being with you. It's this huge charity show and we're woefully under-handed.

EBBA

(Mildly) Short-handed.

MICHELENE

What?

EBBA

Perhaps I could bring her? To the show. She'd love it.

MICHELENE

Ba? No, she wouldn't.

EBBA

She loves clothes.

MICHELENE

Sorry. I've got enough problems.

EBBA

What's the charity?

MICHELENE

Oh, some disease. Look, my job is to ...

EBBA

I know, thoughtless of me.

MICHELENE

You'd better go and see what she's doing. Your room seems to be full of clothes. God knows what she's getting up to ...

EBBA

Oh Lord, I forgot! Natalya's in there ... I'll have to put Ba in the other ...

EBBA rushes out, bowling over CAROLLE, hovering in the doorway.

CAROLLE

(From the door) Sorry. Your door was open.

MICHELENE

Carolle! How's the article coming? I had a word with Ginette.

CAROLLE

Giselle.

MICHELENE

What? Oh. Anyway, we thought perhaps a little more ...

CAROLLE

She said. More depth. My acupuncturist is just round the corner, so ... kill two birds ...

ACT ONE

MICHELENE

Good thinking. Ebba loves your style ...

BA – Ebba's handicapped sister – enters, wearing a mushroom hat.

MICHELENE

Christ Almighty! Take it off, what are you doing?
(She snatches the hat from BA, making her stagger.) I left it in the hatbox in the hall. You'd think it was safe enough there!

EBBA enters.

MICHELENE

She's been at my hat!

EBBA

Oh, it's gorgeous. Sorry. Ba.

BA smiles.

EBBA

I've put you in the back room. Jack and I'll go in the attic. I don't want you going up that ladder.

BA

I oh iy. *(I don't mind.)*

EBBA

No darling.

BA

I oh or roo. *(I want your room.)*

MICHELENE

I honestly don't think it's wise, the way you ... well, she's your sister.

BA picks up her large swatches.

MICHELENE

Don't! They have to go back to Nina's in a reasonable state.

BA

(Frightened) I'm a people person.

CAROLLE seems disturbed by all this. She hovers uncertainly, sits by BA on the sofa, dithers, and offers her a cigarette.

MICHELENE

Oh Pl-ease!

CAROLLE

They are low tar.

EBBA crosses firmly with a cigarette lighter.

BA lights up with difficulty, puffs proudly.

CAROLLE

Sorry, I ... I mean I never smoke myself. These are my analyst's.

BA has noticed NATALYA, curled up, apart. She's fascinated by her red shoes. NATALYA takes them off. BA takes them and puts them on.

EBBA

Oh sorry ... didn't know you were here. Natalya ... Michelene Whelan. Michelene's with my publisher.

NATALYA

(She inspects MICHELENE coolly.) This one marries your brother?

EBBA

Natalya's visiting, from Moscow.

ACT ONE

MICHELENE

Really? Social or business?

NATALYA

I cannot answer. *(MICHELENE is baffled.)*

MICHELENE

(To EBBA) I'm going berserk. Nothing distressed as I asked. Curtain poles with fat ends instead of thin ones. I had a nightmare last night that Emile was putting up wallpaper – figured, embossed wallpaper! I'm supposed to be lunching with the Duchess – our patron – if she shows, and if this is still wearable – *(glaring at her hat)*.

NATALYA

Hah.

MICHELENE

I'm sorry, I didn't get your name ...

NATALYA

I am the Princess Natalya Ivanovna Dubetskoy.

MICHELENE

Oh. How do you do?

NATALYA

Don't curtsey. We are here informally. To see your Queen.

EBBA chokes on her Evian water.

NATALYA

Please be seated. Tell me of this residence you repaint, it is where ... Scotland? Norfolk? Not Ireland, I hope – is for hyippies.

MICHELENE

Surrey.

EBBA

Home counties.

MICHELENE

My fiancé needs to be near the Imperial College, in London. He is an eminent scientist.

But NATALYA is flipping through MICHELENE's fabric samples.

NATALYA

No ... no ... no ... Who is your decorator? You must fire heem. In Venice, I use only silk velvet, colour of little rabbit's bum – and grey silk voile, same colour as canals ... then splash of red. I have this cabinet from the house of Peggy Guggenheim, left to my aunt, against that the Picasso, and the rest, white. We repaint nine times for this white. Then colour is good for all times of day and evening. So important, for the flattering of women. *(She leans forward, peers into MICHELENE's face.)* Ah, you 'ave neglect your skeen!

MICHELENE sits abruptly.

NATALYA

I must go. I need to talk with Richard Branson, he asks to borrow little aeroplane, but he can't have. I need. *(to MICHELENE)* Also remember for making old water-stains, scratch marks on doors, Labradors ... oil from guns. And with water closets, only Victorian. Mahogany, brass ... to be polished. And funny drawings on walls, and pictures of parents looking silly in hats and skirts tucked into knickers for bathing. But also screen by Hockney, maybe bunches

ACT ONE

of ballet shoes. I get these for you from Kirov. But not signed. You take and smell, and say, oh, this is Irek. This is Altynai. Ahh! Your pearls!

MICHELENE

(Clutching her throat) What?

NATALYA

They are not rill!

MICHELENE

(Faint) Cultured.

NATALYA

Tarrible.

MICHELENE backs out of the room, making a daft sort of obeisance.

EBBA

Natale!

NATALYA shrugs. Then she turns her attention to CAROLLE, who looks like a rabbit caught in headlights.

NATALYA

And what are you?

CAROLLE

A journalist.

NATALYA

With humility. That is good.

EBBA

Carolle writes short stories.

NATALYA

Help her!

EBBA looks at NATALYA, surprised. She turns to CAROLLE.

CAROLLE

I dropped by for some extra info. My editor's, you know ... rather ...

EBBA

A bully. Come on.

EBBA Leads her out.

CAROLLE

Could I use your shower? Mine's on the blink.

BA gets to her feet in the red shoes.

She walks about, gingerly at first. NATALYA claps as she begins to get the hang of it.

NATALYA

So – Ba-bar-a ... what do you want?

BA looks down at her severely.

BA

I want to be a bride. *(She says this very clearly.)*

NATALYA

To be married?

BA

Nuh. Be a bride.

She circles in the shoes, and then, as NATALYA looks away, hobbles off quickly with her booty.

NATALYA laughs, and stretches out on the sofa, displaying her legs.

She is not wearing knickers.

Enter BRIAN, in a nondescript suit, no tie.

ACT ONE

BRIAN

Hullo.

NATALYA sits up, and looks at him.

NATALYA

You must be brother. Brain ... but spelt different.

BRIAN

I'm Brian.

NATALYA leaves. BRIAN follows her off.

BA tries to dance in the red shoes to lazy COUNTRY MUSIC.

She totters, topples – kicks off the shoes and dances barefoot, tossing her hair to the beat. She lifts her arms in enjoyment.

Lights change.

ACT ONE – SCENE FIVE

The Living Room.

EBBA and JACK are relaxing on the sofa.

JACK

How was the book signing?

EBBA

Horrible as ever. I kept catching this little man's eye at the back of the queue. He never stopped staring. By the time he got to the table, I felt like taking my top off for him.

JACK

I'll kill the bastard. *(Nuzzles her.)* So – there was a queue?

EBBA

Oh yes. All morning.

JACK

She's good, Michelene.

EBBA

Yes.

JACK

Great publicist.

EBBA

Yes.

JACK

Somebody has to do it.

EBBA

Do they?

JACK

(Sings) 'Money makes the world go round.'

EBBA

What about art for art's sake?

JACK

Wrong century.

NATALYA enters with BRIAN.

NATALYA

This man is rapist. I am concussed. Ebba, pliz, I need bath with oil and everything nice. Come and talk ... wicked man!

She goes. EBBA shrugs, and follows.

JACK

Didn't know you were seeing Natalya. How's it going?

ACT ONE

BRIAN

All right.

JACK

Pretty stunning, don't you think? There's something unusual... something other... about her.

BRIAN

Oh, that's just because her mind's not on it.

JACK

Oh? *(Laughs.)*

BRIAN

Prossies are all the same.

JACK

Prossies?

BRIAN

Prostitutes. The good-looking ones are never any good.

JACK

What?

BRIAN

Still, very professional woman. Doesn't waste time.

JACK

Christ. Bugger me. Can't believe you go in for that sort of thing.

BRIAN

(Simply) I haven't got time to take women out to dinner.

JACK

Sure, but I mean, you don't seem ... How did you get into it?

BRIAN

A friend of mine. We used to go fishing. I went round to see him one night. Couldn't raise anybody. Tried the back door. Next minute, his Mum had me flat on the eiderdown. Ten quid. There's always a back door with a little woman. It's good. You know where you are.

JACK

Yes ... yes, I can see. I mean, I've never thought of paying for it myself. Still. Well. There you are. How about now, though?

BRIAN

Now?

JACK

Now that you're getting married. Will you give them up ... the prossies?

BRIAN

(*Thinks, then*) No. No, I shouldn't think so.

JACK

Won't she mind? Michelene?

BRIAN

Michelene?

JACK

Michelene. The woman you're going to marry.

BRIAN

(*Vague*) Oh ... yes ...

ACT ONE

JACK

You are going to ... marry her. She is under that impression. The arrangements on her side appear to be pretty well advanced.

BRIAN

Really?

JACK

Look ... Brian ... If you're not convinced that nuptials with the Maid Michelene are a good idea, shouldn't you ... ?

BRIAN

No, it's all right.

JACK

So long as you're sure about it.

BRIAN

If it's what she wants. It seems to be what she's after.

JACK

How about you?

BRIAN

Mmm. Did you know they built married quarters on campus in the Sixties in America?

JACK, puzzled, shakes his head.

BRIAN

To encourage breeding. You need 130-plus IQs for astrophysics. Now we need brains for biology.

JACK

So, you want to marry in order to have ... ?

BRIAN

Jack, very soon I shall be able to keep you alive for 300 years.

JACK

Yeah? Hmmn.

BRIAN

What?

JACK

If you'd been able to do that, 100 years ago, Queen Victoria would still be on the throne.

BRIAN waves this away.

JACK

Ebba says you need a new generation every 20 years to stop it all getting ossified and corrupt.

BRIAN

(*Dismissive*) Oh, Ebba.

JACK

Bright lady, your sister.

BRIAN

She's arts!

JACK

So?

BRIAN

Not where it's at. Not since Newton. Science is truth.

JACK

If you say so. And Michelene fits in to all this, huh?

ACT ONE

BRIAN

She'll do. It's either her or some other woman. She's competent, and she won't get into my head, which is a plus. Granted she's a shitbag...

JACK

Natalya certainly thinks so.

BRIAN

What does she know about it? It's not for layabouts and adolescents, marriage.

JACK

Too grown-up for me, I'm telling you.

Lights down on mainstage.

Lights up, down right.

MICHELENE is trying on her veil – over the face – off the face. She decides on off as, when it's over her face, she bumps into things.

She ticks it off her list on her big pink pad, and sits at her dressing table to go through her list.

Enter BA.

She crosses quietly behind MICHELINE – sees her pale jacket – slips it on with a quick look at MICHELENE. Then she sees her smart handbag, seizes it with a grunty groan of pleasure, and runs off.

MICHELINE looks round.

Lights down, down right.

Lights up, down left.

CAROLLE sits alone, watching BRIEF ENCOUNTER on TV. She sips from a mug of cocoa and sobs into a man's handkerchief.

> *Light change.*

ACT ONE – SCENE SIX

The Bathroom.

EBBA and NATALYA are in the bathroom.

NATALYA
You have aperient? I had big lunch and forgot to ... *(Mimes putting her fingers down her throat and being sick).*

EBBA
Natalya!

NATALYA
Actually, I did not forget. But I was not with toothbrush. You must brush teeth after vomit or stomach acid melts enamel.

EBBA
Ugh!

NATALYA
(Points at EBBA.) What size?

EBBA
Twelve.

NATALYA
Ten is better. To be fat is not acceptable.

ACT ONE

EBBA

Neither's shoplifting, lying, cheating and fraud.

NATALYA

Ebba – you are a liberal!

EBBA

There is such a thing as decency.

NATALYA

There is such a thing as survival. Come to bed.

EBBA

Nothing but a bloody tealeaf you are, matey. And you tried to seduce me. Which you are rotten at.

NATALYA

You would know, uh?

EBBA

Yes!

NATALYA

I am exciting for you.

EBBA

Bollocks. You climb into my bed and, when I push you out, you climb back in, drink my Evian water and snore your head off.

NATALYA

I snore?!

EBBA

No. But you do talk in your sleep.

NATALYA

(Alarmed) What? What do I say? What? *(Shakes EBBA.)* What do I say?!

EBBA

Natale! It's in Russian!

NATALYA

Oh. Okay. That's okay. Sorry.

EBBA

There's a lot about you we don't know, isn't there?

NATALYA shrugs, and smiles charmingly.

EBBA

You turn up here, having married my lover. You pinch my man, my bed ... worst of all, my books! I don't know why I don't put on the one pair of shoes – the yellow winkle-pickers, bought when I was stoned – that you haven't scuffed – and give you a smart, hard kick in the vagina. The only reason I don't is ... I can't make up my mind. Are you straight, or are you crooked? Totally true, or totally and utterly false? There is one thing I do know ...

NATALYA looks up sharply.

EBBA

You, my Tartar friend, are up shit creek. And you are frightened. I think very frightened about something. Now don't seek to make moral profit out of my liberal concern just because I'm on to you. You don't have to tell me a damn thing. It might, I daresay, be a hell of a lot wiser for me not to know what you're up to – where you're coming from and why. On the other hand, I am your friend and benefactor, and I am trustworthy.

NATALYA

(Slight pause.) My brother is in trouble. He needs to leave Russia. The money I sent is for him.

ACT ONE

EBBA

The ten thousand?

NATALYA

Is not sufficient.

EBBA

How much do you need?

NATALYA

A lot. I have seen your papers. You do not have enough.

EBBA

(Reacts to this snooping, but rallies.) So, you need to get him out. Well, that shouldn't be impossible. Does he speak English?

NATALYA

Yes.

EBBA

I'll talk to Jack. We'll sponsor him as a translator ... a new English version of Tolstoy ... Gogol ... Pushkin.

NATALYA

You can do this?

EBBA

I should think so.

NATALYA

I owe you much debt. I was thinking, maybe he could marry Ba-bar-a? But ...

EBBA

No, he couldn't. Bad enough waiting for you to leave it long enough not to look phony before you divorce Jack.

NATALYA

Bring Shura here, I am in your debt forever.

EBBA

What has he done?

NATALYA

He is foolish boy.

EBBA

Not the Mafia?

NATALYA

Oh them. I work for them. Pussycats. These is sods from Chechnya. Putin should get wise with those thugs. *(She takes out a PISTOL.)* If you must ... use this. But no. They are for making with cruel, and torturing people. I love my brother.

EBBA

Is that loaded?

NATALYA

(Waving gun about.) You are safe. *(Throws it in EBBA's lap)* Replica. For frighten. *(She looks hard at EBBA.)* Ebba, bring him here. I will repay. I promise.

EBBA

You're actually saying something you mean.

NATALYA

It is serious business. Help me. I will do for you big, big favour.

EBBA

I don't need big, big favour.

ACT ONE

NATALYA

Who knows? Maybe you will.

Lights down on main stage

Lights on, up left.

BRIAN, in his lab, in a white coat, hums cheerily, reading print-outs.

Lights on, up right.

In JACK's office, MICHELENE is bending over a desk, and getting a quick seeing to from JACK.

The FAX spews out a message.

JACK leans sideways – reads. He yelps.

MICHELENE turns her head.

He rips off the fax, holds it in front of her. And they both whoop with glee at the message.

Lights change.

ACT ONE – SCENE SEVEN

The Café Violet.

At lunch are EBBA, NATALYA and BA. They eat in silence.

BA, head down, eats with concentration and enjoyment. EBBA refills BA's glass with pink lemonade.

CAROLLE enters, sees them, and crosses to join them.

CAROLLE

Hi.

NATALYA

EBBA

Hullo.

CAROLLE

Having lunch?

EBBA

Ah ... yes.

NATALYA

(Grabs CAROLLE by the arm.) You got them?

CAROLLE dives in her huge bag. She pulls out and waves TICKETS.

NATALYA

(To EBBA) For Ba and me.

CAROLLE

Tickets for the charity show.

EBBA

Oh Natalya! *(To BA)* Carolle's got tickets! You can go to the fashion show!

BA

Good. Fuck Michelene.

They laugh.

EBBA

Ba! *(To CAROLLE)* Thanks, Carolle. I know they've been like gold – with the Princess coming.

BA

I be Princess.

NATALYA

Of course, darling. We find you wonderful dress ... big jewels ...

ACT ONE

BA

Lots.

NATALYA

So many you can't walk.

BA

That's no good.

NATALYA

I'm joking.

BA

Oh. *(Her hands are sticky, she wipes them in the tablecloth.)*

EBBA

Ba! Use your head!

So, BA wipes her hands on her head.

They laugh.

BA bends her head to her food, then looks up abruptly.

BA

Why haven't I got a boyfriend?

EBBA and NATALYA look at each other.

NATALYA

Ah, who needs it?

BA

(Simply) I do.

An awkward silence.

CAROLLE clears her throat, and turns to EBBA.

CAROLLE

You were going to give me some tips ... about writing ...

EBBA

Oh. Yes. I'm a bit tied up at the moment.

NATALYA

Help her.

EBBA grimaces at her.

NATALYA

Ba. We buy hat.

BA gets up.

BA and NATALYA leave. BA takes her food with her.

CAROLLE leans forward, expectant.

EBBA

Oh. Ah, would you like something to drink?

CAROLLE puts on her 'drinks decision' face.

EBBA

Never mind. Have some Evian. *(Pours for CAROLLE.)*

A WAITER passes by.

CAROLLE

(Waving at WAITER) They know me here. I'd like it with a dash of Perrier? Or, if they haven't got Perrier, just a splash – a smidgen – of Malvern water.

She waves frantically. The WAITER walks the other way.

EBBA tries to think of something to say.

EBBA

We were going to ... You were going to tell me about ...

ACT ONE

CAROLLE

Yes.

Silence. EBBA makes to start. Sighs and stops.

CAROLLE

I realise ...

EBBA

Sure. *(Has a go)* You want to ... ah ... write?

CAROLLE

Yes.

EBBA

Apart from journalism.

CAROLLE

I'm never going to get anywhere with that. Let's face it. It's who you know. And legs.

EBBA

Surely that's true whatever you ... *(She catches CAROLLE's eye, and shuts up. Pause.)* Now. Let's see. What books do you like? Thrillers?

CAROLLE

If they're not too gory.

EBBA

Adventure?

CAROLLE

Not really.

EBBA

Love stories? Joanna Trollope? Rose Tremain?

CAROLLE

Oh yes.

                    EBBA

Anita Brookner?

CAROLLE pulls a face.

                    EBBA

Bit of a downer?

                    CAROLLE

What's wrong with happy endings? It *is* fiction.

The WAITER leans over, refills their glasses with Evian.

                    EBBA
(After an awkward silence.) Being a writer is a lonely life.

                    CAROLLE

Not for you.

                    EBBA

That's because you don't see me when I'm working. *(Thoughtfully)* They do say it helps if you've known pain.

                    CAROLLE

Pain? My editor says I look like something that's happened to Julia Roberts.

EBBA laughs.

                    CAROLLE

I did have an idea. About a woman.

                    EBBA

Go on . . .

                    CAROLLE

About a woman who looks after her mother. Then the mother leaves.

ACT ONE

EBBA

Did your mother leave?

CAROLLE

Yes. *(Slight pause)* She was very good-looking.

EBBA

Your father?

CAROLLE

He was always afraid she would walk out.

EBBA

Write it. Write the story.

CAROLLE

I don't know how it ends.

EBBA

Good. It can end the way you want.

Enter MICHELENE and JACK, both grinning broadly.

EBBA

What are you doing here?

JACK

Three guesses.

MICHELENE

In the bag!

EBBA

What?

JACK

It's happened!

MICHELENE

One big happy family! Tara! *(Does a twirl.)*

EBBA

What's happened?

JACK

Lamarr Wainthrop. Taken over you, me ... amalgamating seven companies under the Wainthrop umbrella. We're all part of the biggest international publishing consortium on the globe.

MICHELENE

Celebration time!

CAROLLE hovers.

MICHELENE

Hullo, Carolle.

CAROLLE

Wow! May I do a feature?

The WAITER approaches.

MICHELENE

Ring my office. Waiter, could we have a bottle of champagne? Krug?

NATALYA appears with BA, who is wearing a colourful new shortie coat with silver dangly bits, and carrying a striped hat box.

BA

Hi guys. What's cooking?

She pulls a grotesque face at MICHELENE.

MICHELENE

Huh?

BA

(*Hisses*) I'm in my element.

ACT ONE

MICHELENE

Has she been drinking?

JACK

(To NATALYA) Celebration! We've just been taken over by Mr Big. Lamarr Wainthrop. The czar of publishing. Where's the champagne?

NATALYA

Fantastisch! My husband! *(Kisses him.)*

CAROLLE

Won't it mean shake-out?

JACK

Possibly. Probably. But it means bigger capitalization. Wider circulation. Better deals for all our clients. *(Hugs EBBA.)* Darling – if you want that place on a windy beach with a leaky beach hut. Room for a mansion out back ...

The WAITER serves champagne.

EBBA

This is good?

BA knocks hers back, and gets a refill from the WAITER

NATALYA

More money?

JACK

Yes. Yes! *(To each.)*

EBBA

(To MICHELENE) You think so?

MICHELENE

Way of the world. Publishing as Gentlemen's Relish?
For the birds!

EBBA

If you can't beat them, join them.

MICHELENE

Absolutely!

JACK

Art's always been dependent on patrons. Kings.
Emperors ...

BA holds her glass out to NATALYA for more champagne.

MICHELENE

... now it's press barons.

CAROLLE

There's sure to be shake out.

MICHELENE

To Lamarr Wainthrop! God bless his Y-fronts.
Health and happiness to all who sail in the new ship
Conglomerate! Yoohoo!

BA spews up all over MICHELENE.

Lights up on BRIAN'S LAB.

BRIAN enters his lab, and switches on the light.

There is a projector. He switches it on, and projects slides of wriggling WORMS. He twiddles the knob till he gets a close-up of a worm.

BRIAN

Oh, you beautiful creature!

ACT ONE

He sits, leaning forward, gazing at the close-up of the worm.

Lights up on CAROLLE'S Room.

In her corner, CAROLLE sits, slumped in her chair, depressed.

She turns on the television, can't stand the loud chatter, turns it off, and just sits.

Light change.

ACT ONE – SCENE EIGHT

The Living Room. Night.

JACK, in a dinner jacket, is pacing.

JACK

(Calls) Come on!

MICHELENE enters in full taffeta, one leg bare to the thigh.

She poses for his verdict.

JACK

Yeah! Catch up with that later. *(Calls)* Ebba!

EBBA enters, looking beautiful.

JACK

Woo-woo!

EBBA

Shut up.

MICHELENE

You see? She can when she wants.

JACK takes their wraps from MICHELENE, and hustles them out.

JACK

Come on, we're late …

Fade to black.

ACT ONE – SCENE NINE

The Living Room – Later.

EBBA and JACK. They are in the same clothes.

JACK

I can't believe it. Usually he's pretty foxy. He's like a lot of these money guys, he's sharp enough to keep his trap shut. But he never stopped talking to you. What was he saying?

EBBA

We were talking about birds.

JACK

Birds?

EBBA

He was brought up near the seashore, like Bri and me. Funny when you grow up by the sea. Makes you claustrophobic inland.

JACK

Did he say that?

EBBA

Yes. I said I felt the same.

JACK

You were on the terrace for ages. Did he come on to you?

ACT ONE

EBBA

No.

JACK

What about you?

EBBA

Me?

JACK

Yah. Do you find him attractive?

EBBA

(Shrugs) For an older man, there's the aphrodisiac of success. The power thing.

JACK

Rattle of the wallet turns you on, huh?

EBBA

No, but I recognise it.

He kisses her.

EBBA

Is he married?

JACK

Not now. Number three wasn't the Mama Mia he was hoping for. He wants children.

EBBA

Children?

JACK

Yup.

The telephone rings. JACK answers it.

JACK

Yeah, oh, hullo sir. Yes, she is. Certainly. *(He switches on the speaker.)*

WAINTHROP (V/O)
(A very pleasant deep American's voice.) Miss Marriner?

EBBA
(Starts with surprise then moves nearer mike) Mr Wainthrop?

WAINTHROP (V/O)
I wondered if you were free for lunch tomorrow?

EBBA
(Looks at JACK) Well, I ... I don't ...

JACK nods at her urgently.

EBBA
Yes, I think I could manage that.

WAINTHROP (V/O)
Kind of you. I appreciate it. Twelve forty-five? I'll send a car.

EBBA
Thank you.

WAINTHROP (V/O)
Good night. *(Rings off.)*

JACK
You see?

EBBA
No, I don't.

ACT ONE

JACK

It's great.

EBBA

No, it isn't. Get me out of it!

Light change.

ACT ONE – SCENE TEN

The Living Room – Later.

EBBA is alone, brooding.

NATALYA enters.

NATALYA

What is wrong?

EBBA

Nothing.

NATALYA

Why do you cry?

EBBA

I'm being silly.

NATALYA

No. Not silly. You cry for your man?

EBBA

No! I was listening to the radio. It was about the war.

NATALYA

You cry for your country? This is shit.

EBBA

Thank you. Thanks very much. What do you cry for?

NATALYA

For me.

EBBA

Fuck off about my country being shit.

NATALYA

It is shit, imperialist pig. Is over for you. Bye bye. The little fingers of Indonesia. Philippines takes your biscuit, and soon China has the trade of all the world by long nails ... *(She gestures.)*

EBBA

Shut ... up.

NATALYA

And you, little piddle island, is nowhere. No power now. Even Wales, which is raining and no coal mines left, is wishing to be free and have romance and fable of itself. You could not even fight. What Englishman would fight as we Russians fought at Stalingrad? All are brain-drain and gone. Who is left to defend you? You are shit.

EBBA

Oh Natalya. You're homesick!

Light change.

ACT ONE – SCENE ELEVEN

Lights up on MICHELENE'S Office.

MICHELENE

(Dialling out. She gets an answering machine.) Ohh! Brian. This is the fourth message. Will you – repeat

ACT ONE

will you – either pick up or contact me asap. Do you want the American refrigerator with the larger ice- making machine? And are we to turn the north room into a gymnasium? If so, I need your input. Otherwise, Emile suggests a studio – art-wise – or a dark room. I'm presuming you don't want a customized laboratory. I can't make all these decisions on my own. Oh, and would you transfer another five thousand into the joint account?

Lights up on CAROLLE'S Room.

CAROLLE

(On the telephone) News desk, please ... Carolle Carpenter for Simon Chance ... .Simon. It's definite. I babysat the handicapped sister last night. The Marriner house ... Yes. Ebba Marriner and Lamarr Wainthrop. They went to the minimalist exhibition at the Tate, and then Claridges ... .Not until 1.50am. I left them making coffee in the kitchen ... Yes, just the two of them ... Thanks very much. Of course, I will. I'm hoping for an exclusive ... Well, if you insist.

Lights up on NATALYA on her cell phone.

NATALYA

(On the telephone) Hullo? *(Laughs)* If you like. Of course, why should I mind? Oh, you are funny. Maybe ... maybe. Oh, you are demand. I see you in one hour, okay?

Lights up on BRIAN's laboratory.

BRIAN brushes his hair with two brushes, wets it down with something from a test-tube after smelling it.

A DISCO. Flashing lights.

BA dances in wild ecstasy.

At one point, head-shaking, she ricks her neck, and staggers, pulling a cross face. But she recovers and dances even more wildly, arching and bending.

Fade to black.

ACT ONE - SCENE THIRTEEN

The Living Room.

JACK and EBBA sit apart in silence. There is tension between them. He makes to speak, but changes his mind.

The DOORBELL rings.

Neither answers it. It rings again. She glares at him. He frowns, gets up. And lets in MICHELENE.

                    MICHELENE

Where is she?

                    EBBA

Who?

                    MICHELENE

The Russian!

                    EBBA

I don't know. I'm not her keeper.

                    JACK

She took Ba to the shops.

                    MICHELENE

Did you know?

ACT ONE

EBBA

Know what?

MICHELENE

About her ... and Brian.

EBBA

No.

JACK

Yes.

MICHELENE

You knew! (*To EBBA*) You knew she'd been seeing him?!

EBBA

No.

JACK

I ... well ...

MICHELENE

Was it your idea?

EBBA

No.

MICHELENE

Obviously, you feel she's a better match. Russian royalty ...

JACK

Royalty?

MICHELENE

(*Out of face*) If one is to believe her.

JACK

(*Laughs*) Natalya?

MICHELENE

I've seen her emeralds. And the brooch with the Romanov crest. She was trying to flog it to Princess Michael. Are you saying you don't know what's been going on?

EBBA

Michelene – I never know what's going on!

MICHELENE

(*Brandishing her left hand with the engagement ring*) Well, if he thinks he's getting this back he's reading the wrong label. I'll flog it first.

EBBA

Have you two fallen out?

MICHELENE

Hasn't he told you? He's broken off our engagement!

EBBA

What?

JACK

He's cancelled the wedding?

MICHELENE

So it seems.

JACK

Because of Natalya?

MICHELENE

I presume so. Apparently, he took her down to Surrey to see the house.

JACK

... and she pissed on it?

ACT ONE

MICHELENE

No! She said it was charming, and hoped he'd be very happy (*Through her teeth*). For some reason... for some reason it's put him off!

EBBA

Good grief.

JACK

Baffling.

EBBA

I expect it's just...

JACK

He'll probably come round. Give it time. Natalya has an effect on people.

MICHELENE

Well I'm not standing for it. And you can make that clear to her. What is she planning to do? Divorce you and marry him? It's ridiculous. I can't make head nor tail of it all. Goddam it, it's only Brian!

EBBA

I'm sorry? What did you say?

MICHELENE

I didn't mean it like that.

EBBA

Yes, you did. Michelene. You caught Brian at a weak moment when he was exhausted after three years of punishing work. He saw you making a prat of yourself in public, and felt sorry for you.

JACK

Eb...

MICHELENE

Whose side are you on?

EBBA

Nobody's. Not even my own, as far as I can see.

MICHELENE

Well, he's not backing out now. If I were to cost my time alone! I've taken your sister off your hands three times!

EBBA

Only once on your own – and you said that was a disaster.

MICHELENE

She spat on a woman's head!

EBBA

Because she made fun of her.

MICHELENE

So, what was I supposed to do?

EBBA

(Tired) I don't know.

MICHELENE

Let's face it. It's not everyone would want to marry into a family with ...

EBBA

With what? With what, Michelene?

JACK

Eb ...

EBBA

(To MICHELENE.) Why don't you just clear off?

ACT ONE

JACK

Ebba!

MICHELENE

This is ridiculous. Where *is* Brian?

JACK

I don't know.

EBBA

Get out of my house.

MICHELENE turns and goes. Sound of a door slamming.

Silence.

JACK

(Laughs.) Natalya and Brian! She's giving us all a seeing to. Except you of course. Look, where were we? All I'm saying is ...

EBBA

I heard what you said. I still can't believe it, but I heard it clearly enough. *(She rises, stands over him.)* You're a pimp. I've been sharing all my secrets with a pimp!

JACK

I'm being realistic.

EBBA

You're being opportunistic.

JACK

Yes, if you must. This is the world we live in!

EBBA

There is no 'world we live in.' Only the world we make. *We* make up.

JACK

Sorry, I do not share your idealism. I'm out there, in that world. You are not. Because I'm out there, you're able to do what you do ... protected.

EBBA

Exploited.

JACK

Protected. By me. You're the best. I honour that. I'm prepared to give you my life. To be the back-up.

EBBA

But not to have children with me.

JACK

Which is why Lamarr Wainthrop is such a beautiful solution for us. Goddam it, Ebba! You're a woman with a heart. Lamarr Wainthrop's had his broken. His first wife dies in childbirth. He marries again. His wife miscarries till she gets fed up and runs. He marries a fertile-looking Italian who turns out to be a harpy. And then he meets you. You can give him what he wants. A couple of kids. Then an amicable divorce. Meanwhile, I stay in the background.

EBBA

We are not in the same universe. How could I have believed we were? You persuaded me that to be a salesman was an honest job. I've admired you for doing what I couldn't. Face people. Make deals. I've been grateful. Now, I ask myself, has the job done this to you? Or was I mistaken? Were you always a pander? I should have seen it. She told me.

ACT ONE

JACK

Natalya?

EBBA

No. The journalist. 'He's not prepared to commit.'

Silence.

JACK

Ebba! Come on. There's no mileage in it any more. Dad? Head of the family? Women and children first? You don't need our protection any more. The honour code is cracked to pieces. I can't give you what you want.

EBBA

You mean you won't?

JACK

I can do better. I can turn you towards it.

EBBA

I'm to marry one of the richest men in the world and give him children so that you can prosper in his conglomerate. Have influence over him, over me. You're ambitious, Jack.

JACK

Will you at least think about what I've said? Give it realistic thought. It needn't make any difference to us!

EBBA

The fact that you can say that is a knife thrust I shall never recover from.

NATALYA enters with BA.

Silence.

BA looks from EBBA to JACK and back to EBBA.

>   BA
>
> I been fucked.

>   *Blackout.*

ACT ONE – SCENE FOURTEEN

Livin Room. A little later.

EBBA, JACK and NATALYA.

EBBA and NATALYA are arguing.

>   EBBA
>
> I don't believe you!

>   NATALYA
>
> She was always in my eyes!

>   EBBA
>
> It's a dive! You'd no business taking her there.

>   NATALYA
>
> She likes to dance.

>   EBBA
>
> Ba doesn't tell lies. If she says ...

>   NATALYA
>
> She doesn't know what means to be fucked.

>   EBBA
>
> Of course she knows.

ACT ONE

NATALYA

Examine her. You will see. She drank one beer, that is all ... maybe two. Maybe mine as well. I don't drink this piss ...

EBBA storms out of the room.

JACK

That's blown it.

NATALYA

(Shrugs.) What if she is fucked?

JACK

Come off it. Has she been?

NATALYA

How should I know? *(Lights up.)*

JACK

Christ Almighty.

NATALYA

Is not true. You know why she says this.

JACK

Why?

NATALYA

(Shrugs) She feels the hate in the room. It makes her mischief.

JACK

Mischievous.

NATALYA

Whatever. She is being wicked. I know this feeling. We share. So, will she marry him? Ebba? The rich man?

JACK

I doubt it.

NATALYA

Hah! Down grade for Jack, hanh?

JACK

You could say so.

NATALYA

What will you do, my husband?

JACK

Cut it out.

NATALYA

I think of something.

JACK

I wish you would. If she could just see. The way I figure it, we could make everyone happy. And find you a billionaire on the side.

NATALYA

Good. *(She smokes, and looks at him shrewdly.)* Did you make arrangement?

JACK

Sorry?

NATALYA

For my brother. To come here.

JACK

Sorry. Haven't had time.

NATALYA

He needs to leave quickly.

ACT ONE

JACK

Okay. I'll see to it.

NATALYA

Please do.

JACK

Look, I've said I'll try. I can't promise anything. I have some calls to make.

JACK grabs his cellphone and goes.

NATALYA looks after him. She sits and thinks.

EBBA enters.

NATALYA

You see? She was joking with you.

EBBA sits heavily.

NATALYA

She is not fucked.

EBBA

(*Mutters*) No, I'm the one who's fucked.

NATALYA

What?

EBBA

You heard me.

NATALYA

Why do you quarrel with your lover?

EBBA

Oh, don't say you don't know. That he hasn't told you. That you haven't heard us yelling all over the house? You think it's a good idea, no doubt, marrying me off.

NATALYA

I don't know. I haven't met him, your rich man.

EBBA broods.

NATALYA

What is he like?

EBBA

Old.

NATALYA

How old?

EBBA

Bloody sixty. *(Slight pause.)* He doesn't look it.

NATALYA

What does he look like?

EBBA

Like a forty-year old tennis player from Australia. *(Gloomily)* He's got his own teeth. Probably capped.

NATALYA

You have been to bed with him?

EBBA shakes her head.

NATALYA

Maybe you should. Not if you don't wish.

EBBA

He's all right. Sane.

NATALYA

Does he have sense of humour?

EBBA

Yes. Yes, he does.

ACT ONE

NATALYA

You see? You are involved already.

EBBA

(Laughs) Not in the way you mean.

BA enters in a kimono, with flowers in her hair.

She twirls lazily, switches on the TV, and watches, with the sound off, on her stomach.

NATALYA

You don't want him?

BA

Wan' who?

NATALYA

This rich man I was telling you, Ba-bar-a. He wants to marry Ebba.

BA

No.

NATALYA

Why not?

BA

She got Jack. *(Goes back to TV.)*

EBBA

I got Jack.

NATALYA

You know what kind of man is Jack.

EBBA

Do I?

NATALYA

You told me, you want children. So – protect them.
My father was wounded in Afghanistan. Useless.
No pension, no money. When you choose a man, you
choose a father for your son, for your daughter. You
cannot be frivolous.

Silence.

EBBA

I take what you say. The trouble is, I have chosen.

NATALYA

Jack.

EBBA

He's everything I most dislike. He's venal,
calculating. But – I've had lovers. A doctor. An
illustrator. An Irish songwriter who went out one day
and never came back ...

NATALYA

Not so many.

EBBA

I'm a romantic. I have to be in love. When I met Jack,
it was like coming home. I knew all about him before
we spoke. I can't go back – start all over again. I'm
ready now. Every month is a little death.

NATALYA

You are a good woman. You are deserving better.

EBBA

Oh, come on! Anyway, he's not *all* rogue. He did marry
you. He's more of a knight errant than he knows, the
silly sod.

ACT ONE

NATALYA

The marriage was illegal.

EBBA

What? What?! *(She bursts out laughing.)*

NATALYA

We tricked him, my brother and me. His Russian is tarrible.

They laugh.

EBBA

Oh, by the way. Your brother. All fixed. *(Takes papers, hands them to NATALYA.)* Airline ticket. I've asked for him asap.

NATALYA takes the papers. She holds them.

NATALYA

I owe you big favour.

EBBA

Oh, rats.

NATALYA

I mean this. *(She thinks.)* You want him ... Jack?

BA

She want Jack. *(Turns back to TV.)*

EBBA

I want Jack.

NATALYA

Okay. I fix for you. When do you see your rich man?

EBBA

I'm supposed to be having dinner with him tonight.

NATALYA

Where?

EBBA

(Pulls a face.) The Ritz.

NATALYA

He will come here?

EBBA

(Shakes her head.) I said I'd join him.

NATALYA

You have hat?

EBBA

Hat?

NATALYA

I need hat. Small. With veil.

BA kicks the hat box across with her foot.

NATALYA

Ba-bar-a. Angelica!

BA

That's not my name.

NATALYA

(Hugs her.) I can wear your hat?

BA

Yuh, but don't mess it up.

NATALYA tries it on. BA offers flowers. They try them.

EBBA shakes her head. The flowers come off.

NATALYA

At what hour the Ritz?

ACT ONE

EBBA

Nine. Don't jump him, it won't work.

NATALYA

Please. I am professional.

EBBA

That's what I'm worried about.

NATALYA

He will think me virgin – a maiden!

EBBA

That I doubt.

BA

(Points to the hat.) Don't break it.

NATALYA

It will come back neat and new as before.

BA

Good. *(Sits up with cross expression.)* I don't want to be a smelly bride, you know.

Light Change

ACT ONE – SCENE FIFTEEN

A Catwalk.

Sounds of preparation. SOFT MUSIC in background.

Standing are: EBBA and NATALYA, their heads together, gossiping.

Enter BRIAN, escorting CAROLLE. They sit separately.

EBBA looks at him surprise, then turns to NATALYA.

EBBA

You could have found him someone more exciting. She's not a great journalist.

NATALYA

But good wide hips.

EBBA

I'd have liked a higher IQ.

NATALYA

No. Your brother will be spurned by a clever woman. He is chauvinist.

She waggles her huge engagement ring across at CAROLLE, who rises, smiling, and comes across to marvel at it.

CAROLLE

Can I see?

NATALYA

Of course.

CAROLLE nods at EBBA.

CAROLLE

Hullo Ebba.

EBBA

Congratulations. You got him away from the laboratory.

CAROLLE

(*Smiling*) I know! (*Examining ring*) Wow! How much did it cost? Do you mind me asking?

NATALYA

Three hundred and fifty thousand pounds. Special price for Mr Wainthrop.

ACT ONE

She lifts CAROLLE's hand, looks at CAROLLE's small engagement ring, drops CAROLLE's hand dismissively.

Enter MICHELENE.

NATALYA

Michelene! Michelene! Come and sit with me.

MICHELENE, seeing them, looks outraged.

CAROLLE returns to BRIAN.

BRIAN waves cordially at MICHELENE.

MICHELENE joins EBBA and NATALYA.

MICHELENE

What are you doing here?

NATALYA

Salabrating.

MICHELENE

(Glaring at BRIAN and CAROLLE.) Don't tell me ... ?

NATALYA

Rebound. After you give him kick out of door.

MICHELENE

I give him ... ? *(She covers.)* Well, second thoughts time. *(To EBBA)* I'm sorry, Ebba. Do hope Brian isn't feeling too bruised.

EBBA

I hear he's given you his share of the house. What are you going to do, sell it?

MICHELENE

I've already done a swap for a Notting Hill five storey with four bathrooms, conservatory, and access to private gardens.

NATALYA
Good condition?

MICHELENE
Not a decent fitting in the place.

NATALYA
I will advise. Aspect?

MICHELENE
Backing south-west.

NATALYA
Very good. Furnish moderne, but not minimal – is crap. Good pictures – but domestic. You are not a gallery. So, nice Euan Uglow girl's bum, Rose Hilton, little Craigie Aitcheson yellow bird. I have also some Russian painters who will be so, so valuable soon. Simple pale walls ... no false marble, no splash about with silly finish. Plain kitchen. Aga I suppose. I will assist.

MICHELENE
Thank you.

NATALYA
But you are still wearing them! *(She yanks at MICHELENE's pearls.)*

MICHELENE
Sorry ...

NATALYA
Jewels must be good!

MICHELENE
That's all very well. I don't have your advantages, Princess.

ACT ONE

NATALYA

You have no money? Look at girls coming from Chelsea Art School. Do they have money? They look sensashonal! Find unfashionable shop in area where they ... what is ... peoples taking in things for money ...

EBBA

Hock shops. Pawnbrokers.

NATALYA

Yah. Look and find. For your skeen – garnets ... many ropes. And yellow topaz, like your eyes. Fire opals to give life to the face. And dye your hair red! Be lively woman. Peacock. And cease to worry. Take a little drugs from time to time. Relax. Maybe find a good protector.

MICHELENE

Where am I going to find a Lamarr Wainthrop, like Ebba?

NATALYA

He is with me now. Ebba is with Jack.

MICHELENE's jaw drops.

NATALYA

For Ebba, moonstones, river pearls. Everything pale. But you. Never again enter chain store – not even for G-string. Cease to be English. Like Americans say – get wise. Make money. You are persistent woman. Sell! Woman who can sell is rich – independent! But first you need ten thousand for the teeth.

MICHELENE

Princess, where am I going to find that sort of money?

NATALYA takes off her engagement ring, hands it to MICHELENE. Who gawps at it.

> EBBA

Natalya!

> NATALYA

Sell it. Get comparative price. Maybe auction? Do it well.

> MICHELENE

I can't take this.

> NATALYA

When the Princess Natalya offers you gift, be gracious to accept.

She waves MICHELENE away imperiously.

MICHELENE totters over to BRIAN and CAROLLE, and shows them the ring. They look across in amazement.

> EBBA

You are mad. Why?

NATALYA shrugs.

> NATALYA

I am sorry for this woman.

> EBBA

Why?!

> NATALYA

She is provincial.

> EBBA

What are you going to say to Lamarr?

> NATALYA

I lost the ring. Buy me another.

ACT ONE

MUSIC up a touch. More NOISE from backstage.

EBBA

I wonder if he'll believe you.

NATALYA

Doesn't matter. Tomorrow I go home.

EBBA

What?

NATALYA

I said, tomorrow I go home. Shura is safe. You brought my brother here. *(She kisses EBBA.)* Better not to sleep with him. He is careless boy.

EBBA

He's adorable. Why are you going back?

NATALYA

I must.

EBBA

Why?

NATALYA

Because nothing is right here. I need her.

EBBA

Your mother?

NATALYA

Mother Russia.

EBBA

Is he going with you? Lamarr?

NATALYA

Nah, nah, nah. I leave early. You will drive me to the airport. Here. Keys of car. For you.

The MUSIC surges. They have to speak up.

EBBA
I don't want your car.

NATALYA
Sell it! Buy good clothes – some shoes ...

EBBA
No way. I'll give the car back to Lamarr. But what shall I say to him?

MUSIC up.

NATALYA
What?

EBBA
What do you want me to tell Lamarr?

NATALYA
Tell him ... Tell him ... Dosvedanya!

MUSIC.

Lights lower.

On a big screen upstage, we see MODELS, showing outré clothes, walking towards us (and back) on the catwalk.

Seated at their tables, BRIAN, CAROLLE, MICHELENE, EBBA and NATALYA watch and applaud – their backs to us.

EBBA and NATALYA rise to applaud a particularly spectacular outfit.

JACK enters, and stands between them, placing a hand on each bum.

BA enters, dressed as a bride.

ACT ONE

Excited by the show, she sashays up and down, imitating the models. Then dances ecstatically to the music.

Fade to black

The End.

LADYBIRD, LADYBIRD

For Sue Parrish

LADYBIRD, LADYBIRD was first performed on April 23rd, 1979, at the King's Head Theatre, Islington, London, UK.

CAST

Mrs Ashley	JANET HENFREY
Christine	CAROLE HARRISON
Kevin	PHILIP CROSKIN
Jenny Fletcher	ANGELA CARROLL
Directed by	SUE PARRISH
Stage Manager	PHILIPPA MOUNTAIN

'Ladybird, Ladybird, fly away home
Your house is on fire.
And your children all gone.'

REVIEWS

"Ladybird, Ladybird" is a gripping, truthful play, which – without making individual accusations – nevertheless indicts our societal structure.

Mrs Ashley (powerfully played by Janet Henfry) has had two sons taken into care. Her schoolgirl daughter and working son, Dan, complete her household. With sure writing and deft direction, the play takes on a reality and atmosphere, setting the scene for the visit of a social worker. Though short, the narrative is forceful and revealing. In addition to Miss Henfry's performance, Carole Harrison, Philip Croskin and Angela Carroll turn in controlled, well-modulated portrayals. Most certainly it should be seen.

Interesting to note: where once O. Henry, Katherine Mansfield and their successors ruled the short story genre, with the decline of that form, the subsequent vacuum has three-dimensionally been filled by the one-act play in this country.

YURI KOHUT. *The Stage*. 03/05/1979

The Gems family are keeping us busy these days. Jonathan has just made his mark at the Bush, while his mother, Pam, is responsible for this extraordinarily spare and touching lunchtime piece at the King's Head. Mrs Ashley (Janet Henfry) lives in a bleak flat with two teenage children. Her younger two boys have been taken into care. Mum is on tablets for her stomach trouble and refuses to see a specialist. A middle-class social worker (Angela Carroll) does not help when she calls round.

It is like the background story to the sort of snippet in the newspaper you can read any day of the week. Miss Gems is a feminist writer to be sure, but she is never raucous. She distills these social problems with such care and sensitivity that their reverberation in our lives is always assured. She is greatly aided by the sympathetic direction of Sue Parrish.

MICHAEL COVENEY. The *Financial Times*. 25/04/1979

PAM GEMS' heartbreaking glimpse into the reality of life for so many women, "Ladybird, Ladybird" is the most moving presentation seen at the Brighton Actor's Workshop theatre at the Sea House in Brighton for many months.

Concerned with a mother depressed to the point of physical illness, it is written with an authenticity and insight that sets the observer pondering the process by which she arrived at the point where we encounter her.

Widowed early, Mrs Ashley lives a drab existence in a degree of poverty and deprivation just sufficient to make her the subject of welfare attention. Her two younger children who live with her, are capable enough, but life for all is overshadowed by her weary inadequacy. Yet she is a woman who could have been happy. She found real happiness in bearing her children and is not lacking intelligence and imagination, but here she is, as Jean Trend presents her in a performance of outstanding quality, a born loser who will inevitably fade deeper into failure and despair.

Jean Trend's portrayal is so good that it is pleasant to find it so ably supported by Barbara Mayne as the woman's proud, impatient daughter; by Gerald Cox as her good-natured son, and by Julia Asling as an earnest and concerned welfare worker.

Directed by Martha Beirne with design by Christine Minshull, this must be numbered amongst Brighton Actor's Workshop's most ambitious and successful presentations.

CHARLES PLUMLEY. *The Stage.* 03/04/1980

LADYBIRD, LADYBIRD

ACT ONE

ACT ONE - SCENE ONE

A living room which goes through into a kitchen.

The MOTHER sits over an electric bar fire, which is not on.

FRANKIE, her daughter, about fifteen, enters in her school uniform. She throws down her shoulder bag of books.

FRANKIE makes herself a cup of tea, and opens cupboards, looking for something to eat. She finds a Cream Cracker at the bottom of a packet and sits down at the living room table. She fishes the teabag out of her cup and drops it on the oilcloth.

Without a word, the MOTHER gets up, picks up the teabag, drops it in a mug in the kitchen, pours hot water over it from the kitchen tap, and returns with her cup to her seat by the fire.

FRANKIE
There's some milk in the bottle.

There is no response. The MOTHER sits, hunched, turned away from her daughter, sipping the hot liquid noisily.

FRANKIE drinks up, but it does not go down well. She chokes slightly, and coughs. When the spasm subsides, she pushes the cup aside, flips open her school books and begins to scribble rapidly.

Her MOTHER turns on a small, battered radio. FRANKIE shifts slightly. She looks briefly across at her MOTHER. Then goes on writing. Finishing with a wild scrawl she slaps her books shut, rises, scraping the chair horribly, and throws on her coat.

> MOTHER
>
> Where you going?
>
> FRANKIE
>
> Out.
>
> MOTHER
>
> Where?
>
> FRANKIE
>
> Round to Jean's. (*They lock stares.*) I'll be back at nine.
>
> MOTHER
>
> I don't care what you do.

She turns away, looking up at the mantelpiece. FRANKIE follows her gaze. There is a letter there.

> FRANKIE
>
> Hey – is that a letter from the kids?

Her MOTHER looks away.

> FRANKIE
>
> How are they? Are they all right?

She waits for an answer. There is none.

> FRANKIE
>
> Can I have a look? (*She approaches the letter tentatively.*) Can I see?

She gives her MOTHER a swift look, takes silence for a yes, and puts her hand up for the letter. There is no remonstration, so she takes it down and reads it. She smiles happily at the news.

ACT ONE

FRANKIE

They seem to be all right ... Yeah ... Doesn't say they feel homesick. It looks as though they're having a good time.

Her MOTHER turns away.

FRANKIE

We-ell ... it gives you a bit of a break. (*She props the letter back carefully.*) Right. Anything you want? There's no bread. Shall I get some bread?

Her MOTHER turns and looks up at her with a petrified face.

FRANKIE

(*Gently*) I'll get some bread, Mum. (*There is no response.*) See you later.

She goes.

The MOTHER sits. She appears to be listening to the radio. Then she gets up and tears the letter violently into small pieces. She turns off the radio and crosses to a cupboard. She pokes about and finds a pot of jam. She brings it back to the centre of the living room and stands there, eating the jam out of the pot with her fingers. Finishing the pot, she wipes her hands on her dress and then stands on a chair. She fetches down a piece of greaseproof paper from the top of the fitment, takes from it a solitary slice of sliced ham, puts on a plate.

She lays a knife and fork, and a bottle of sauce as her son DAN enters.

He is about seventeen and, like his sister, young and comely and full of life.

DAN

Hullo, our Mum!

He throws off his knapsack, takes off his outer jacket, washes his hands under the kitchen tap, and has a deep drink of water.

His MOTHER makes him a cup of tea.

> DAN
>
> Thanks.

He clicks approvingly out of the side of his mouth at her as she stands over him in her old kimono. Her gaze is mild in response.

> DAN
>
> How've you been?

> MOTHER
>
> Not too good.

> DAN
>
> Did you get to work?

She shakes her head.

> DAN
>
> Look, I said . . . Go down the surgery! Tell him you want to see a specialist. Get on to him!

She makes a sneering sound.

> DAN
>
> I would.

> MOTHER
>
> Do you want some ham?

He is surprised at the offer. He turns and sees the thin, unadorned slice of ham on the plate. He pulls a funny face, unseen by his Mother.

> DAN
>
> Thanks.

ACT ONE

He sits at the table. His MOTHER undoes his knapsack, takes out the squashed remains of his midday sandwiches and puts them next to his plate.

She pours the remains of the milk in his tea carefully, to the last drop. He eats. She watches him.

DAN

Where's Frankie?

MOTHER

How should I know? I see you've bruised your knuckles.

DAN

Did she do her homework?

MOTHER

She was scribbling something.

He nods. His sister is home safe.

DAN

She must have done then. (*A pause while he eats.*) Heard anything from the kids?

She does not reply.

DAN

We'll hear soon. As soon as they're settled. What about going down to see them? Do you fancy that?

MOTHER

Where's the money coming from? (*But she gives him a mild look.*)

DAN

If I still had the bike, I could run you down there.

She gives him a mocking look that is almost a grin.

DAN

You think they'd have let us know. A postcard or something. Still, they must be all right. You're getting a rest – that's the main thing.

He looks round vaguely, hoping to light upon something else to eat. He is reaching for his crumpled daily paper as FRANKIE enters with a plastic carrier bag.

She dumps down on to the table a loaf of bread, butter, cheese, milk, biscuits, and a four-pack of beer.

DAN

(*Pleased*) Hey!

MOTHER

What's all this?

FRANKIE

He needs milk for his tea.

MOTHER

Where did this come from?

FRANKIE

The shop – where do you think? At least you can have a decent cup of tea.

MOTHER

(*Quick*) He's had his tea. He's had some ham.

FRANKIE

Oh? Where from? (*To DAN*) Did you bring it back with you?

He shakes his head at her, behind his Mother's back.

MOTHER

I bought it for him.

ACT ONE

FRANKIE

Oh. Thanks. I'm supposed to live on fresh air, I suppose.

MOTHER

You get a school dinner. Danny's earning.

FRANKIE

(*To her MOTHER*) Do you want some bread and cheese?

MOTHER

I don't want anything.

FRANKIE mutters in fury, and leaves the room, banging the door loudly.

DAN falls swiftly on the food.

DAN

You've upset her.

MOTHER

Expects to come in here of a Monday night to a three-course meal, she's got another think coming.

DAN

Leave it.

MOTHER

Where'd she get the money? Coming in here showing off like that. Did you give her any money?

DAN

I gave her a sub this morning.

MOTHER

How much?

DAN

Couple of quid.

MOTHER

What! What for? I won't have her cadging off you.

DAN

Your library fines for one thing. Take the bloody books back on time! (*Slight pause.*) She's got to keep up with the other girls, Mum. She needed some tights.

MOTHER

Oh yes, to gad about in. When she's not sitting with her nose in a book.

DAN

What about you? All I ever see is the top of your two heads.

A VOICE outside the door calls.

VOICE

(*Sing-song tone, bright*) Anybody in? Hullo?

DAN

Somebody at the door.

MOTHER

Sssh!

DAN

Who is it?

MOTHER

(*Urgent*) Sssh!

She gestures for him to stay still.

VOICE

Can I come in?

ACT ONE

DAN

(*Mouths*) They can tell we're in. The light's on.

MOTHER

(*Mouths*) Shut up.

They wait. Silence.

DAN

They've gone I think.

SOCIAL WORKER

(*Outside*) Hullo? Okay if I come in?

DAN, about to sit, jerks to his feet and pulls a face.

His MOTHER moves away, crosses to her corner and leans against the mantelpiece and the wall.

A YOUNG WOMAN enters. She is untidily dressed, with a bulging shoulder bag. She is no great beauty and her hair is boring.

DAN, nonetheless, brightens at the sight of a young female.

DAN

Mum ... Ah ...

JENNY

Hullo, Mrs Ashley. I just wanted to see how ...

MOTHER

What do you want?

JENNY

How have you been? (*To DAN*) Hi. I'm Jenny Fletcher.

DAN

Pleased to meet you.

JENNY

I can't stop, but I just thought I'd pop in to make sure you're okay. Sorry I'm late but there's been the odd crisis. (*To DAN*) Miz Mackintosh is away.

DAN

(*Slightly less warm*) Oh. You're from the borough?

JENNY

(*With a winning grimace*) Right! Have you heard yet ... from the kids? How are they getting on?

DAN

No idea. We haven't heard.

JENNY

Oh, that's funny. It should have arrived by now. We ... Never mind. Tomorrow I expect. (*She turns fully to the MOTHER*) How are you? I hear you've been under the weather ...

MOTHER

What?

JENNY

Under the weather. A bit, you know ... Well ...

The MOTHER and DAN regard her without response.

JENNY

Yes, well ... Silly really. I mean, we're all under the weather if you think about it. Underneath the weather ... (*She trails off.*)

DAN

(*After a silence*) Do you want a cup of tea?

His MOTHER gives him a fearsome glare behind the SOCIAL WORKER's back.

ACT ONE

JENNY

Oh. Mmm, thank you.

Her bright smile indicates she has been drinking tea in four households already. DAN gestures her to a seat. The MOTHER remains standing, propped up against the mantelpiece.

DAN

Mum's not well.

JENNY

Has she seen the ... (*To the MOTHER.*) Have you seen the doctor?

MOTHER

I'm on tablets.

DAN

Do you take sugar?

JENNY

Oh thanks. Three please.

The MOTHER's head turns.

JENNY

No, make that two.

DAN

Sure?

She nods, smiling matily.

DAN

So, been solving all the problems, eh?

JENNY

Trying to.

DAN

Pretty tough.

JENNY

Well, no peace for the wicked.

MOTHER

Who?

JENNY

What? Oh, sorry. I seem to be getting into clichés. Are they doing anything?

MOTHER

What?

JENNY

The tablets. for your ... (*with the fastest glimpse at her file*) ... back?

DAN and his MOTHER look at each other, mystified.

DAN

Back?

JENNY

Wasn't it your ...?

DAN

Mum gets stomach trouble.

Hiatus. A pause.

DAN

So, the kids have settled in okay?

JENNY

Right as rain. (*She catches the MOTHER's remorseless eye.*) Ah. Done it again. I must watch that ... maddening. No, they were looking fine.

MOTHER

(*Slightly startled*) You saw them?

ACT ONE

JENNY

Sorry?

MOTHER

You've seen them? You've seen my kids?

JENNY

Yes! We thought we'd take a break. Pop down to the home. Make sure everybody was okay. It was great. We watched them play football. Brian scored a goal.

MOTHER

What about Sean?

JENNY

Oh, he was ... You know, settling in.

MOTHER

Was he crying?

She stares at the girl, Medusa-faced. The SOCIAL WORKER is unable to deny it, or speak before her face.

MOTHER

He was crying.

Slight pause.

JENNY

They're bound to be a bit homesick at first.

The MOTHER turns away.

JENNY

Shows what a good home they come from if they miss it.

No response.

JENNY

I gave him a cuddle.

Pause.

DAN

How's his asthma?

JENNY

Asthma? (*This baffles her for a second. Then she nods competently.*) Right. (*She uncaps her fountain pen and makes a note. Then looks up with a reassuring grin.*) No, they're settling in really well, honest. It's a super place.

The MOTHER turns suddenly and gives her a terrible, brilliant smile. Again, the SOCIAL WORKER is defeated. She breaks the stillness with a foraging dive into her shoulder bag.

JENNY

Brian sent you this.

She gives the MOTHER a shapeless, coiled brown object, about palm-sized. The MOTHER's hand remains open.

MOTHER

What is it?

JENNY

(*Giggles*) Actually, I'm not too sure! (*To DAN*) They've got a kiln down there. Great facilities for arts and crafts. They've got looms, silk-screens, printing press ... A lot of the local people give voluntary training in their spare time. People are very good. They get the little ones doing modelling. Of course, they're too young to throw pots but they let them put their little bits in the oven.

DAN and MOTHER exchange a glance.

ACT ONE

MOTHER

It looks like a lump of shit to me.

The SOCIAL WORKER decides this is a joke and gives a little shriek of laughter.

DAN, under no such illusion, moves abruptly and takes the object from his MOTHER's hand.

JENNY

We'll have to give him the benefit of the doubt.

DAN

(*Since she shows no sign of going*) More tea?

He gets another glare from his MOTHER.

JENNY

Ooh, no. No thanks. Well, okay – if there's a drop more.

The MOTHER rises as DAN turns to the pot.

She prowls behind the SOCIAL WORKER, grabs the biscuits brought in by Frankie, and shoves them under JENNY's nose.

MOTHER

Biscuit?

JENNY

Ah, no thanks.

MOTHER

(*Tearing savagely at the wrapper.*) I'm sorry I can't offer you anything more substantial. I'm slimming at the moment.

JENNY

Thanks, I've just eaten.

> MOTHER
>
> You sure? They're... (*with a quick glance at the label*) ... Rich Osborne!
>
> DAN
>
> (*Putting down the refilled mug of tea.*) Sorry it's a bit weak.

They watch as she sips from the huge mug. She manages yet another cheerful grin.

> JENNY
>
> Perhaps I'll change my mind.

The MOTHER offers the biscuits promptly. The SOCIAL WORKER takes one.

> MOTHER
>
> Take two. You'll need two with a mug that size. Why didn't you offer her a decent cup, Dan?

DAN looks at her bewildered. They have no cups.

> MOTHER
>
> Have you noticed, Danny? Miss Fletcher's got green eyes.
>
> JENNY
>
> My name's Jenny. I mean, if you want. (*She eats.*)
>
> MOTHER
>
> Go on, take another.
>
> JENNY
>
> Thanks. I'm okay.

ACT ONE

MOTHER

(*To DAN*) She was going on about it last time she came. (*To SOCIAL WORKER*) I thought of you when I was in Woolworths.

DAN

(*Mutters warningly*) Leave it.

MOTHER

No. They had some of them poppit beads. I haven't seen them for ages. They used to be all the rage. I thought: 'Just the thing for that Miss Whatsername. Pondweed green. Isn't that what you said?

She blunders to her feet and seems, for a moment, to be unfocused.

JENNY

Did I? To be honest, I ...

MOTHER

No, I've got them somewhere – if I can find them.

She moves about, knocking things over.

JENNY

It doesn't matter. The next time I look in.

MOTHER

(*Turning for a split second*) Next time? (*She carries on searching, throwing out the contents of a sewing box.*) They're in a plastic bag.

JENNY

Oh, lovely. Perhaps Friday?

MOTHER

... a black, plastic bag.

JENNY

I just wanted you to know that the boys were okay.

MOTHER

... unless *she's* been at them.

JENNY

I must be off.

MOTHER

I remember! I hid them in the lavatory.

She dodges out of the room with a competent and reassuring smile.

JENNY

(*Quickly, to DAN*) How has she been?

DAN

About the same.

JENNY

Has she seen her doctor?

DAN

No. Look, I think you better ...

He jerks his head for her to go, but it is too late. The MOTHER returns with the beads.

MOTHER

Here we are. Look. there, do you see, Dan? It's a lovely match. Stand still.

She puts the beads round the girl's neck, then turns her round for inspection.

MOTHER

No, I think they'll go round again.

She un-pops them and doubles up.

ACT ONE

JENNY

Ooh! That's too tight! I think they're too tight. Could you...?

DAN

They're too tight, Mum! Take them off, you bloody fool. You'll throttle her...

MOTHER

Rubbish, they're only poppets. Just un-pop them and they fall to bits.

JENNY

Oh please... (*She can't get her fingers inside the beads.*)

DAN

Here, stand still. I'll do it. Stand still. I'll just get my finger in...

MOTHER

(*Giggles*) Oh, not your great fingers, Danny. Here.

The SOCIAL WORKER gives a short, gasping scream.

MOTHER

Oh dear. Uncomfy is it? No, you're right. They are a bit tight. I'll get a knife.

She picks up a large carving knife.

JENNY

(*Slowly and carefully*) Mrs Ashley. Put the knife down.

DAN takes the knife and pushes his MOTHER away. He undoes the beads and they fall to the floor.

MOTHER

(*Reasonably*) I was only going to cut her free.

DAN and the SOCIAL WORKER pick up the beads and put them on the table. The MOTHER leans against the mantelpiece.

MOTHER

(*Still reasonably*) When are my kids coming back?

JENNY

Sorry?

MOTHER

Well, you must know. When are you bringing my kids back?

JENNY

I thought you were pleased with the arrangements. Miz Mackintosh said ...

MOTHER

How long are they going to be away?

JENNY

We're making every effort to rehouse you. The idea is for you to have a rest. A sort of holiday.

MOTHER

Holiday.

The SOCIAL WORKER bends to pick up her notebooks.

MOTHER

How far is it?

JENNY

I beg your pardon?

MOTHER

To the home? The place where you've got my kids.

ACT ONE

JENNY

I'm not absolutely sure.

MOTHER

But you've been there. You've seen them.

JENNY

It's part of my job.

MOTHER

Oh well, in that case. (*She sits suddenly, as if losing energy and interest.*)

The SOCIAL WORKER puts her things together. She takes her shoulder bag from the chair, preparing to go.

The MOTHER grins to herself, and laughs slightly.

MOTHER

Did I ever tell you? I always remember ... (*She laughs.*)

DAN

What?

MOTHER

When you were born?

DAN

No, you never. Did I make it?

MOTHER

Matter of opinion.

JENNY

Could I just ... ?

She reaches for the rest of her things on the table.

MOTHER

It was in U.C.H. University College Hospital. We were living near King's Cross at the time. Before they pulled it all down. Your father was with a carpet firm. Can I offer you a glass of beer? Danny, get a glass.

DAN looks among the debris in the kitchen.

MOTHER

Don't worry. I'll have mine in a cup.

She throws her tea dregs across the room, narrowly missing the SOCIAL WORKER.

MOTHER

My daughter popped back with some shopping for me. She's just gone round to see a school friend. Biscuit?

The SOCIAL WORKER is forced to sit again. She shakes her head at the biscuit, but takes a large glass of beer from DAN.

MOTHER

Anyway, what was I saying?

DAN

When you were in hospital.

MOTHER

Oh yes. Oh Lord, yes. First view you ever got of the world was those overhead lights. Screeching bright lights. Tiled walls and green masks. It's no wonder kids like science fiction! No. An interesting day. I wanted a boy. I don't know why. I wonder why that is?

DAN

What?

MOTHER

Mothers and sons.

ACT ONE

She looks at him. He grins genially – then at the SOCIAL WORKER.

MOTHER

Anyway, they were going to induce me. Get you going. You were overdue. I was frightened. I was only a kid. I thought they meant you were dead. And they don't tell you. Anyway, as luck would have it, you decided to arrive at one am. They'd just bedded me down. I was popular, I can tell you. What's more, as it turned out, you *were* born dead. They'd given me too much pethidine, not realising you were almost there, and it stopped your heart. They lifted me up to watch you being born. For some reason, you were on your back. It's like trying to shit a brick with the lav on the wall. Of course, out you came with a swoosh, all grey and dead. Not that I realised. They whipped you off somewhere. I could hear them muttering and scurrying around cursing to themselves. A nice young Chinese student did the delivery. It was his first. He kept looking up my way to ask if I was orr light. Then he couldn't find the vein to inject the stuff to get the afterbirth away, so they gave me a whacking great punch in the stomach. Anyway ... After they'd mucked about with you for a bit, I heard this sort of little gasp. This little sort of choke.

DAN

And that was me?

MOTHER

I couldn't believe it. I couldn't believe it. I got a good look at you while they were talking. They put you on a trolley quite close. You had a tube up your nose. Oxygen. They'd wrapped you in this bit of old

blanket. Blue. Anyway, it was close enough for me to
see you. Weird really. Your ears were all bent down.
You had no chin. I don't know where your chin was.
There were red marks all over your head and you
were yellow. You were jaundiced they told me after.
I couldn't get it straight. I was dopey with the gas
and air. First the Chinese student, then this Chinese
baby. Your eyes were all slitted up with the drug. The
pethidine. Then, all of a sudden, they whisked me off
to the pre-theatre room where they put the Caesars.
They were short of beds. I sat up and waited for you. I
was as wide-awake as a toad and ever so hungry, but
of course there was nothin' doing that time of night.
And, when they didn't bring you, I thought: hullo.
What's up? What's wrong? I sat up listening to the
hot water pipes, and watching the clock on the wall.
You can imagine what I thought. I'd given you up
altogether, except I didn't want to ask. I wanted to put
off knowing. You can see why they kill messengers
with bad news. Anyway. I was too frightened to ring
the bell. I did in the end and, oh dear, did I get told off.
'You'll have to wait. We've got forty babies to see to.'
I couldn't help thinking, well, I'll take one off your
hands. Just bring me mine. Of course, I still thought
you were dead, and they weren't telling me. By this
time, my nipples were dribbling all down the front of
my gown. I was so embarrassed. And I was getting
these terrible contractions, where I wanted you. In
the end, I got up. I had to. I didn't care. I couldn't help
it. I could hear you crying somewhere. I got a short
answer for that. I thought they were goin' to lock me
in.

ACT ONE

JENNY

They were probably short-staffed.

MOTHER

Oh, I've no complaints about their efficiency. They were very efficient. I'm efficient myself.

She looks around the chaotic room.

DAN

So ... did you ever get me?

MOTHER

Well, I suppose it was you. You were still swaddled up in the bit of blue blanket. Your head looked like a black bean. It was wringing wet. The blanket. Where you'd been crying. 'What's this?' I said. 'Oh, he's been naughty. He's been a noisy boy, haven't you? He's had a whole bottle of water already.' I was sitting there, soaking, and they'd stuck a piece of rubber in your mouth.

The SOCIAL WORKER rises quietly.

JENNY

(Gently) I must be going.

MOTHER

Like your father's last day. I didn't know, you know. I had no warning. Everything was going along. Normal. All of a sudden. Stop. Nothing.Finish. Nothing at all. Like the blind man I saw being interviewed on telly once. They asked him what it was like, being blind. (*She gives a scoffing, soundless laugh, lifting her head.*) 'I suppose it's all dark,' says the interviewer. 'No, no,' says the blind man. 'It's not dark. No, no.' 'Oh, what's it like then?' says the interviewer. 'What is there?' 'Nothing,' says the blind man. 'There's nothing. Nothing at all.'

She drinks deeply from her cup of beer.

> MOTHER
>
> Have you got a boyfriend?
>
> JENNY
>
> No, not at the moment.
>
> MOTHER
>
> Pretty girl like you, I should think they'd be queuing up.
>
> JENNY
>
> I don't have much time.
>
> MOTHER
>
> No life of your own?
>
> JENNY
>
> I get pretty tired.
>
> MOTHER
>
> Now, that's something Geoff never was. He worked very long hours. On the go all day. And the worry, well, we never had enough money. Still, just the same, all our children were conceived in rapture. No planning. Oh no. We-ell, never the right time, is it? Look at the price of a pram. Never mind a roof over your head. Not to mention the inconvenience. I mean, you've just finished growing up ... got it together, with a bit of know-how and elegance. All of a sudden, straight back to everything smelling of widdle. I remember changing Brian's nappy once. We were out in the car, and I was using a disposable. I went to

ACT ONE

throw it out of Geoff's window, which was open, and gave him a shit moustache.

DAN snorts into his beer.

MOTHER

I can't think why we went in for you all really. Geoff used to say it was his contribution to society. Providing energy units. People look at you really funny if you go in for children nowadays. They think you're Catholic, or daft. Or that he's gay and wants to keep you quiet. You get some funny looks. And told off – if they think you can't afford it, and it's gonna come out of their taxes. I often wonder why we did it. I mean, it wasn't just to have you. Geoff hated the idea of owning things. He said it was just another word for maintenance. And you know how good he was at that! He wouldn't even say my son, my daughter. 'They're not mine,' he used to say. 'They're their own. They belong to themselves. He just wanted people to be with. It's natural. (*She drinks.*) We were as bad as each other. I'd have had half a dozen – just to see what came out. I like babies. (*Turns to the Social Worker*) Do you know what I really like? Naming them. Choosing names. I really love that. Not that we didn't always settle for something safe in the end. I've always been fond of the name Violet. But it's not fashionable nowadays. People don't go in for violets much. Are you going to have any?

JENNY

I haven't really thought about it.

MOTHER

How old are you?

JENNY

Twenty-six.

MOTHER

And you haven't thought about it?

JENNY

There are so many people in the world already.

MOTHER

Yes. I keep hearing that. Well, don't leave it too late. You haven't got forever.

JENNY

To be honest, I've never had the urge.

MOTHER

Oh, you don't get that till you've had the first. Of course, in the old days, people got started willy-nilly. Now, with being able to choose ... Geoff used to say that, with the Pill – and being able to get out of it – in the end, only motherly and fatherly people would end up having kids. So, eventually, they'd be the only sort left. The other thieving buggers would go extinct.

DAN gives a short bark of laughter.

JENNY

It's such an awful responsibility.

MOTHER

You're looking after children, aren't you?

JENNY

Yes, but they're not my own.

MOTHER

No. You can get off the boat and throw away the paddle any time you want.

ACT ONE

JENNY

I beg your pardon?

MOTHER

What about his asthma?

JENNY

Sorry? What?

MOTHER

Standing around on a bloody football pitch in this weather.

JENNY

Oh. Well ... Look, I'm sorry. This is really Miz Mackintosh's case.

MOTHER

Case. D'you hear that, Dan? Case.

JENNY

We do our best.

The MOTHER turns in her chair violently, and leans over, craning towards DAN.

MOTHER

Do you know what she said to me? The other one. The old one. When I wouldn't sign the bit of paper. She stood there and said: 'Of course, from our point of view, it really would be easier if the boys were in care. (*She heaves a huge, theatrical sigh.*) I was being a nuisance, not wanting to get rid of you all so's they could do their jobs. I felt like saying 'Am I affecting your livelihood? Sorry. Shall I cut me ear off, give you something to be going on with?'

She tips the edge of the SOCIAL WORKER's files, almost toppling them. The SOCIAL WORKER makes a saving grab.

> **MOTHER**
> Then there was the one before that. With the twitch. And the one before her. The one who never stopped grumbling about the price of everything, and not being able to get a decent flat. Poor thing. She felt it affected her work. She had to go back to Sunderland in the end and do electronics.

Enter FRANKIE.

> **MOTHER**
> Shut the bloody door!

FRANKIE turns, slams the door, and takes off her coat.

> **FRANKIE**
> Who's this?

> **JENNY**
> Jenny Fletcher.

> **FRANKIE**
> Oh?

> **JENNY**
> I'm a social worker.

> **FRANKIE**
> Oh. One of them. How are the kids?

> **JENNY**
> Fine. They're looking very well.

> **FRANKIE**
> Oh, you've seen them?

ACT ONE

JENNY

I saw them yesterday. They're settling in nicely.

FRANKIE

Yeah, we got the letter.

There are looks all round. DAN fills the breach after an open-mouthed scowl from his MOTHER.

DAN

Brian made this.

He proffers the BROWN OBJECT.

FRANKIE

What's it supposed to be?

The MOTHER grasps her midriff and doubles over in violent pain. She makes repetitive, loud, animal grunts, going into a howl. The sounds are awful, too loud, inhuman and frightening.

FRANKIE

Christ Almighty!

FRANKIE wrests the slopping cup of beer from her MOTHER's hand.

DAN

What's up, Mum?

JENNY

Are you all right, Mrs Ashley?

The MOTHER howls and writhes, clutching her abdomen.

JENNY

What is it?

DAN

She said she'd had stomach ache ... Mum?

The MOTHER begins to groan. The sounds are now softer, not so terrifying. They stand round her.

FRANKIE

(*Apart*) Oh, leave her alone.

DAN

What is it?

FRANKIE approaches her MOTHER.

FRANKIE

Come on. You'd better lie down.

JENNY

She seems quite ill. Shouldn't you call a doctor?

FRANKIE

(*Helping her Mother out of the room*) You got some funny ideas.

We can hear the MOTHER being sick outside.

FRANKIE returns.

DAN

What do you think, Fran?

The SOCIAL WORKER moves anxiously. FRANKIE stops her from going to the Mother.

FRANKIE

She's better on her own.

JENNY

(*To DAN*) I do think, the doctor ...

DAN

(To *FRANKIE*) What do you think?

ACT ONE

FRANKIE

Leave her alone, for God's sake.

JENNY

I'm sorry but I think we must do something. She sounds very distressed.

DAN

She did say she'd been feeling bad.

FRANKIE

Look, for Christ's sake, leave her alone! Leave it!

She sits down heavily in the broken armchair, at a distance from them.

FRANKIE

She'll be all right in a minute.

JENNY

Perhaps I'd better wait. Just in case.

FRANKIE gives her a look of contempt, then turns away and opens a paperback, cracking the spine.

JENNY

(*To DAN*) We'll see how she is in a minute.

DAN

(*Nods*) I suppose you ... Ah, you see quite a lot, eh? Different problems.

JENNY

We haven't got the facilities we'd like.

DAN

No, well ... same all over.

JENNY

Most of the time it's just a question of holding the fort, clearing the decks.

DAN

Why, you in the navy?

Slight pause.

DAN

What made you go in for it?

JENNY

Sorry?

DAN

This sort of work.

JENNY

I wanted to help people.

Slight pause.

FRANKIE

(*Shouts at her Mother*) You okay out there?

There is a muffled reply. The sounds of someone being sick subside. The MOTHER appears at the door, worse for wear. She looks smaller and is trembling slightly.

FRANKIE rises.

FRANKIE

Get a towel, Dan.

FRANKIE crosses to the sink, runs water in the washing-up bowl, and picks up soap and a raggy flannel.

The SOCIAL WORKER finds a towel and gives it to DAN.

ACT ONE

DAN

Thanks.

FRANKIE begins to clean her MOTHER, and sponge the sick off her.

FRANKIE

I shouldn't have brought that beer in. I knew I was making a mistake.

MOTHER

(*Mumbles*) It went down the wrong way. Mind!

She flinches as FRANKIE washes her face.

FRANKIE

You'll have to take this off. It stinks.

DAN

Have a lie down, Mum.

FRANKIE empties the bowl, rinses it out and hands it back to the MOTHER.

FRANKIE

Here, you better take this in case you're sick again. Where's your book?

DAN reaches over and picks up a book.

DAN

Here.

MOTHER

No, not that one. The other one. The one about Margot Fonteyn.

The SOCIAL WORKER finds it and gives it to DAN, who gives it to FRANKIE, who gives it to her MOTHER.

DAN

Here, I'll take her. Do you want a cup of tea?

                              FRANKIE

I'll bring you some aspirin later on. Let her stomach
settle first.

                              MOTHER

Can I have the fire?

DAN unplugs the electric fire and picks it up. Then he takes his
MOTHER out.

FRANKIE crosses and sits in her MOTHER's chair. She picks up
her book.

                              JENNY

Has she had spasms like this before?

FRANKIE ignores her. The SOCIAL WORKER makes a note in her
case history.

                              JENNY

Let me know how she goes on.

FRANKIE doesn't answer.

                              JENNY

Perhaps you'd give me a ring? I'll write my number
down for you.

She proffers the piece of paper with the telephone number, but
FRANKIE ignores her, and carries on reading.

The SOCIAL WORKER puts the piece of paper on the table, tucking
it under the bottle of tomato sauce.

                              JENNY

I've left it on the table.

FRANKIE continues to read.

                              JENNY

Is there anything I can do for you?

ACT ONE

FRANKIE turns a page.

> **JENNY**
> You're sure there's nothing you need?

There is no response.

> **JENNY**
> Good-night then. I'll be going.

Still no response from FRANKIE.

> **JENNY**
> Good-night.

She turns at the door.

> **JENNY**
> I hope your mother feels better soon. If not, do telephone.

She pauses for a moment, but FRANKIE continues to read without acknowledgment.

The SOCIAL WORKER leaves.

FRANKIE moves her head briefly, noting her departure, and carries on reading.

Fade to black.

The End.

Also from Quota Books . . .

PAM GEMS
PLAYS ONE

THE INCORRUPTIBLE
GARIBALDI, SI!
THE TREAT

*

PAM GEMS
PLAYS TWO

GO WEST YOUNG WOMAN
NELSON
NOT JOAN THE MUSICAL
KING LUDWIG OF BAVARIA

*

PAM GEMS
PLAYS THREE

BETTY'S WONDERFUL
CHRISTMAS
THE SOCIALISTS
GUINEVERE
ETHEL

*

PAM GEMS
PLAYS FOUR

FRANZ INTO APRIL
PASIONARIA
AUNT MARY
LADYBIRD, LADYBIRD

*

PAM GEMS
PLAYS SIX

DEBORAH'S DAUGHTER
FINCHIE'S WAR
AT THE WINDOW
STELLA CAMPBELL

*

PAM GEMS
PLAYS SEVEN

MY WARREN
THE AMIABLE COURTSHIP
THE ODD WOMEN
CEDRIC AND LOUISE

*

PAM GEMS
PLAYS EIGHT

THE FATHER
DANCE OF DEATH
THREE SISTERS
STANLEY'S WOMEN

*

PAM GEMS
PLAYS NINE

A DOLL'S HOUSE
GHOSTS
HEDDA GABLER
AFTER BIRTHDAY

Q

Available from: www.quotabooks.com

Q

website: www.quotabooks.com
email: info@quotabooks.com
Twitter: @Quotabooks

www.ingramcontent.com/pod-product-compliance
Lightning Source LLC
Chambersburg PA
CBHW050207130526
44590CB00043B/3019